We **Love** desserts! And Marlene Koch really knows how to *LIGHTEN UP* those deliciously sweet recipes! *Unbelievable Desserts with Splenda* offers mouthwatering rich and creamy desserts that can guiltlessly be enjoyed by all! That's why we choose it to be the first selection of our book club! Thanks Marlene!
— *Janette and Christina, hosts of Lighten Up! As seen on The Food Network*

With Americans averaging 31 teaspoons of sugar a day, it's time to get serious about cutting back! *Unbelievable Desserts with Splenda* helps you do that, with mouth-watering desserts that are just as sweet with little or no sugar. From old favorites, such as Hot Chocolate, Blueberry Muffins, and Chocolate Chip Cookies to more adventuresome recipes, such as Chocolate Almond Torte, Key Lime Cheesecake, and Strawberry Soufflé, this book lets you have your cake and eat it, too . . . without the calories and sugar!
— Elizabeth Somer, M.A., R.D., author of *Food & Mood* and *The Origin Diet*

A godsend to diabetics, weight watchers, and all healthy eaters who still have a sweet tooth. Use this cookbook, enjoy it, and be healthy!
— Nancy Lorraine, Midwest Book Review

You will not believe these recipes are so low in sugar. Not only do I eat these desserts myself, I am proud to serve them to my guests.
— James Decker, Certified Executive Chef, The Lakes Golf and Country Club, Sous Chef, Team USA. International Culinary Olympics

Low-Sugar baking has never been better. The delicious recipes, ranging from Amazing Creampuffs to Unbelievable Chocolate Cake, fit easily into diabetes or low-calorie meal plans with taste and portion sizes that truly satisfy. This book is loaded with sound nutrition information, great recipes, and creative baking tips.
— Krista Kriegal, MS, RD, Certified Diabetes Educator

If you are diabetic or care about someone who is, *Unbelievable Desserts with Splenda* should be an essential part of your cookbook library.
— Review from Epinions.com

This is an excellent book to satisfy any cravings you might have for sweets. It has just about anything you could need to satisfy those sweet craving. I highly recommend this book. — Review from Low Cal Diner.com

Fantastic Food with Splenda

160 GREAT RECIPES FOR MEALS
LOW IN SUGAR, CARBOHYDRATES,
FAT, AND CALORIES

Marlene Koch

Illustrations by Christopher Dollbaum

M. Evans and Company, Inc.
New York

M. Evans and Company, Inc.
216 East 49th Street
New York, NY 10017

Library of Congress Cataloging-in-Publication Data

Koch, Marlene.
  Fantastic food with Splenda : 160 great recipes for meals low in sugar, carbohydrates,
  fat, and calories / Marlene Koch ; illustrations by Christopher Dollbaum.
    p. cm.
  1. Cookery. 2. Nonnutritive sweeteners. 3. Sugar-free diet—Recipes.
  4. Low-carbohydrate diet—Recipes. I. Title.
TX714.K63 2003   641.563837—dc22   2003016617

Book design and type formatting by Bernard Schleifer
Manufactured in the United States of America
ISBN 1-59077-021-8 (hardcover)
10

Life is Fantastic—Enjoy!

Contents

Acknowledgments

As in any project, many thanks are due. First—to my great boys, Stephen and James, for their patience (or as much as they could muster) upon hearing me say, one more time, that I had to work "on the book" again (and again . . .). And to my husband, Chuck, for giving me all the support and needed space to get it done.

"Getting it done" was no small feat, especially considering a large move thrown into the mix, but three fantastic assistants helped to make it happen. A big thanks to Sara, my upbeat kitchen assistant, who never wavered despite some terrific messes. To Chef Laura Johanson—I never believed much in fate, but I can't describe why else we met. To have a professional pastry chef from the Culinary Institute of America, who just happened to be interested in low-sugar baking, able to jump in on a day's notice with great professionalism and attitude while I was furiously working on the desserts—with a tight deadline. . . . You have a long and great career ahead, of that I am sure. And to Christine Sardo, M.P.H., R.D.—thank you and thank you again. Hours and hours of tireless help—typing, editing, refining, printing—with a smile to boot (even in the wee hours)! If anyone is listening, this is definitely someone you want to work for you!

I am fortunate to have a fantastic editor in P. J. Dempsey, who makes my job as easy as it can be from a publishing perspective. Thanks for the continued wonderful support and friendship. I would also like to thank the rest of the team at M. Evans for their work and support. Most especially to George de Kay, who passed away this year—you were always fair, always supportive, and *always* a gentleman.

I would also like to take this opportunity to extend my thanks to all the wonderful supporters of my work who helped to make my first book a success and this one possible: Jacqueline Carranza at McNeil Nutritionals, Christina Deyo and Janette Barber from *Lighten Up!* on the Food Network, Connie Cahill, executive chefs James and Erica Decker, Lisa Drayer from dietwatch.com, Lynn Grieger from ivillage.com, Kristi Morris, Deb Lackey, Julie Horner and Teresa Pangan from Puttin' on the Web, and the numerous others who gave great support both in person and through encouraging and positive e-mails.

Last, but not least, I extend my thanks to family and friends who make everything possible. I can't give enough thanks to my parents, who are always there for me (even in subzero temperatures), and my lifelong friend Nancie, who always gives exactly what I need. And, most especially, to my brother and talented illustrator Christopher Dollbaum—thank you for taking this on. I am certain it is more than you bargained for, but so worth it (especially to me!).

Introduction

TWO YEARS AGO I WROTE MY FIRST COOKBOOK, *Unbelievable Desserts with Splenda—Sweet Treats Low in Sugar, Fat, and Calories*, because I was convinced I had finally found the secret to producing delicious, yet healthy, low-sugar desserts. Since that time I have had the fortunate opportunity to speak to thousands of people, from students at cooking schools and chefs at industry meetings to health professionals at trade shows and consumers at health fairs. Across the board, I am pleased to say the response has been simply wonderful, even from the toughest critics (the chefs, of course). So, first and foremost, I would like to thank all of you—especially those of you who recommended my cookbook to patients, colleagues, friends, and family. I want to tell you how much your enjoyment and endorsement of the book means to me.

For those who asked, "What about other foods, recipes beyond desserts?" I dedicate this book to you. Because while desserts and sweet beverages are the obvious foods we think of that are filled with sugar, they are not alone. Breakfast foods, salads, vegetables, condiments, and even some entreés contribute significant amounts of sugar and excessive carbohydrates to the diet. What's terrific is that Splenda works just as well to flavor a variety of foods as it does to sweeten desserts. If what you crave is "real food" like Oven Baked French Toast, Sweet and Sour Chicken, Maple Sugar Baked Beans, and Cranberry Sauce—delicious and sweet but without the calories or carbs of sugar—this book is for you.

But do not panic: I have not forgotten you "sweet treat" fans (like me). For us, I have included lots of tasty new desserts and beverages for every occasion. There are all-new recipes for frozen desserts like ice cream and sorbet, as well as traditional favorites like rich egg nog, creamy custards, and old-fashioned puddings. It was my goal to try and come up with guilt-free versions of all your favorite foods so that you can enjoy them again even if you're watching the sugar, carbs, fat, or calories in your diet.

I have also included the basic information so many of you told me you found invaluable. This basic information incorporates the facts and tips about cooking and baking with Splenda and professional nutritional analysis on each recipe, including the much-requested calculations for Weight Watchers[ww] Points. In addition, you'll find suggested variations on many recipes along with an understanding of why I've chosen to use specific ingredients (and what are acceptable substitutes). If I've done my job well, you'll not only be able to recreate the recipes, you'll also be knowledgeable enough to experiment on your own. To help you, I've broken down the different types of advice into the following categories:

Chef's Tip

Food Trivia

Nutrition Fact

PART I

NUTRITION
INFORMATION

Frequently Asked Questions about Splenda

MY INTEREST IN SPLENDA CAME ABOUT BECAUSE I FIND IT TO BE THE BEST tasting, safest, and most versatile sugar substitute on the market today. I am a consumer of the product just like anyone else. I do not profit from your purchase of Splenda. Over the past few years, I have been asked many questions about the product, so here I'll take the time to answer the most frequently asked questions and provide you with an understanding of why Splenda works, tastes great, and is safe to eat.

What *is* Splenda?

Splenda is actually the brand name for the nonnutritive sweetener sucralose, the only no-calorie sweetener made from sugar. Sucralose is made from sugar through a patented multistep process that selectively replaces three hydrogen-oxygen groups on the sugar molecule with three chlorine atoms. The result is an exceptionally stable and intense sweetener that tastes like sugar but lacks sugar's calories and any of the aftertaste found in some sugar substitutes. Sucralose is then mixed with maltodextrin (a natural bulking agent) in small amounts to create Splenda packets (each equivalent to the sweetness of two teaspoons of sugar) or, in larger amounts, to create Splenda Granular, which measures cup for cup like sugar.

Is Splenda safe?

Over one-hundred studies have been done in the last twenty years to confirm Splenda's safety. It is approved by the FDA for use by everyone, including pregnant women and children. Splenda carries no warning labels and does not have any undesirable side effects. It has also been recognized as a safe sugar alternative by consumer advocates and health authorities, including the Center for Science in the Public Interest, physicians, and holistic health professionals (including many who do not advocate the use of other sugar substitutes).

Does Splenda add calories or carbs to food?

Although sucralose has no calories or carbohydrates and Splenda packets contain zero calories, Splenda Granular does contain 96 calories per cup and 24 grams of carbohydrate (from the maltodextrin used to bulk sucralose so that it measures one to one for sugar). Compare this to granulated sugar with 775 calories and 192 grams of carbohydrate per cup!

Will Splenda affect blood sugar or raise insulin levels?

Unlike with other sugars, such as sucrose, lactose, glucose, and even fructose (sometimes referred to as the "oses"), the body does not recognize or metabolize sucralose as a carbohydrate; therefore, it does not create an insulin response, raise blood sugar, or affect triglycerides.

What are the benefits from using Splenda in recipes instead of sugar?

Recipes made with Splenda offer a delicious and healthy alternative for people who need a:

- Reduced-sugar or low-carb diet, including those with diabetes or on the Atkins diet
- Reduced-fat diet, including those with heart disease
- Controlled-calorie diet, including those on Weight Watchers
- Healthy but delicious diet they can live on!

What Is It about Sugar?

Sweet or Sour?

ONCE ONLY KNOWN FOR SIMPLY BEING SWEET, SUGAR HAS BECOME A media sensation. Sugar has been used in greater amounts by food manufacturers over the last decade not only to entice our palates but also to sweeten their profits. Lately, though, we've experienced the current wave of diet books that are sour on sugar and want us to believe that it is the root of *all* our health woes. What's the real scoop?

The *Scoop* on Sugar

The scoop is that sugar has many incredible properties that truly enhance the flavor, texture, and appearance of the foods we eat. Humans are born with a natural sweet tooth, so it's no surprise that high-sugar foods are popular. To be fair, many studies have indicated that small amounts of added sugars (see "Added Sugar" chart below) in a healthy diet are not harmful to our health. What is harmful is that our diets tend *not* to be healthy and our sugar consumption is anything *but* small. In fact, consumption of refined sugars has soared in the last decade. The typical American now consumes up to 18 percent of his or her total calories from added sugars, for a total of 170 pounds per person per year! Scientific evidence supports that sugar consumed at these levels can contribute to dental caries, increased triglycerides, insulin resistance (which contributes to weight gain and diabetes), and obesity— even in healthy individuals. And for the 17 million Americans with diabetes or the estimated 30 million already with insulin resistance, the negative side effects of too much sugar are even more pronounced. Not completely soured on simple sugars, the USDA, along with more than forty respected health organizations, simply recommends that we limit added sugars to no more than 10 percent of our total calories or 10 teaspoons a day for a 2,000 calorie diet (or as little as 7 teaspoons for 1,600 calories). But when you consider that a piece of banana cream pie can have 14 teaspoons of added sugar (*not* counting the milk sugar or the banana), a coffeehouse chai tea 10 teaspoons, and even the holiday favorite cranberry sauce 10 teaspoons of added sugar, it's easy to see how we all end up eating too much sugar.

The Sweet Solution

My solution is to reduce sugar in your diet without eliminating the sweet foods you love. With this book you can do just that. Here you will find Banana Cream Pie, Indian Chai Tea, and Two-way Cranberry Sauce. By using Splenda in these recipes you will reduce the amount of sugar in each serving to a single teaspoon. So, whether you are limiting sugar or the carbs from sugar, my recipes will allow you to cut the sugar while you still enjoy the sweet taste and maintain your health. In addition, you'll also benefit from cutting sugar's unwanted calories. That's what I call sweet!

Fat—Friend or Foe?

REMEMBER, NOT SO LONG AGO, WHEN CARBS WERE GOOD AND FAT WAS bad? It now appears the pendulum has swung the other way—but maybe not as far as you think.

Low-Fat and Lean = Healthy Weight Loss

Let's be realistic—fat, like sugar, makes food taste good. In fact, if I didn't limit the fat content in my recipes (as in some low-carb cookbooks), developing great-tasting low-sugar recipes would be easy. But these high-fat recipes would also be contrary to what we know about the impact of fat on your health (and your weight). Here's why:

First, fat is full of calories and, yes, calories still count. The scientific support for low-calorie diets that lead to weight loss are numerous, as are the many commercially available weight-loss programs based on this fact. Because 1 gram of fat, healthy or not, equals 9 calories, whereas protein and carbohydrates are each only 4 calories per gram, high-fat diets are often high in calories (and made even higher when you pair the fat with sugar).

Second, eating large amounts of fat, especially saturated fat, can also lead to greater insulin resistance, which contributes to weight gain.

Third, extensive studies clearly implicate saturated fat, and now trans fat, in increasing the risk of heart disease and certain cancers. This risk is especially significant when you consider that people who are obese, are insulin resistant, or suffer from diabetes are already at increased risk for heart disease.

Low-Fat and Luscious

Therefore, based on what we know, the experts overwhelmingly recommend moderating the amount of fat in our diet. Cutting fat is hard, but there are ways to do it without cutting the fat completely and without sacrificing the taste of the foods you crave. Consider the following:

The Dietary Guidelines for Americans, the American Heart Association and American Diabetes Association, along with many protein-based diets like The Zone, advise that no more than 30 percent of your daily calories come from fat, with saturated and/or trans fat accounting for no more than 10 percent. This equals approximately 65 grams for someone consuming 2,000 calories a day, or as little as 50 grams for 1,600 calories a day (often the amount required for weight loss in women). To put that in perspective, a single serving of Three Bean Salad can contain 20 grams, a scone from a coffeehouse can have up to 28 grams of fat, and luscious chocolate mousse can have over 40 grams of fat!

Now just imagine—Three Bean Salad, only 6.5 grams of healthy fat (page 102); a Blueberry Scone with only 4 grams of fat (page 69); and luscious Dark Chocolate Mousse with a mere 5.5 grams of fat (page 191). And not only is the total fat low in these recipes, but so are the saturated fat, trans fat, and calories! But most important is these fantastic foods still taste great!

Diabetes

Diabetes—The Epidemic

I T SEEMS EVERYONE NOW KNOWS SOMEONE WITH DIABETES—A RELATIVE, A friend or even themselves. My stepdaughter has diabetes, as does one of my aunts and several colleagues. Almost 17 million Americans have diabetes, and this number is expected to rise 50 percent by the year 2025. If you do not know someone who has diabetes now, you will soon.

Diabetes—The Carbohydrate Connection

Eating too much sugar does not *give* you diabetes. There are actually many factors involved, some unknown (especially with type 1) and some very clear, like the increased risk for type 2 diabetes due to obesity, inactivity, and genetics. Whatever the cause, once you have diabetes, controlling the amount of carbohydrates in your diet becomes an important tool in regulating blood sugar, which is crucial because the disease manifests itself by disabling the mechanisms needed for the body to metabolize sugars properly. These sugars come from eating carbohydrates, whether complex, like whole grains, which raise blood sugar slowly, or simple, like sugars, which have the ability to quickly "spike" blood sugar. Even though the American Diabetes Association allows *both* types of carbohydrates in a healthy diet, the total combined amount must be kept at an appropriate level to keep blood sugar in check. Since simple sugars are very dense in carbohydrates, and yet devoid of fiber and nutrients, problems can arise when too many of them are consumed. The bottom line is, a person with diabetes must develop a carbohydrate budget for each meal and each day, and sugary foods are very hard on the budget!

Fantastic Foods for Diabetes

Because the fantastic foods in this book are all low in carbohydrates, fat, and calories, you can eat many more of the foods you love along with a variety to choose from at each meal. So, even if your diet is restricted because of health issues or because you want to cut calories and take off (or not gain) a couple of extra pounds, you can use the recipes in this book to do it without sacrificing either quality or taste. Isn't that fantastic?

(Read on and see just how much you save.)

The Fantastic Food with Splenda Difference

Breakfast

High Protein Cinnamon Pancakes (page 74), 3 4-inch

Apple Cider Butter Syrup (page 266), 3 tablespoons

Calories 345
Carbs 40 grams
Fiber 2 grams
Fat 11 grams
Protein 22 grams

Diabetic exchange = 2½ Carbohydrates, 3 Lean Meat
WW point comparison = 7 points

Compare to:
Pancakes, 3 4-inch

Maple syrup, 3 tablespoons

Butter, 3 pats

Calories 550
Carbs 93 grams
Fiber 3 grams
Fat 19 grams
Protein 6 grams

Diabetic exchange = 6½ Carbohydrates, 3 Fat
WW point comparison = 14 points

Save: 205 calories, 53 grams carbs, 8 grams fat, and 7 points

Gain: 3 grams fiber, 16 grams protein

Lunch

Barbequed Pork Sandwich (page 163)

Sweet and Sour Party Slaw (page 110), 1 cup

Bread and Butter Pickles (page 158), 5 slices

Calories 335
Carbs 40 grams
Fiber 7 grams
Fat 12 grams
Protein 22 grams

Diabetic exchange = 2½ Carbohydrates, 3 Lean Meat
WW point comparison = 7 points

Compare to:

Barbecued pork sandwich

Sweet-and-sour coleslaw, 1 cup

Bread-and-butter Pickles, 5 slices

Calories 650
Carbs 75 grams
Fiber 4 grams
Fat 33 grams
Protein 15 grams

Diabetic exchange = 5 Carbohydrates, 2 Medium-fat meat, 3 Fat
WW point comparison= 16 points

Save: 315 calories, 35 grams carbs, 21 grams fat, and 9 points

Gain: 3 grams fiber, 7 grams protein

Holiday Dinner

Turkey Breast, 4 ounces

Two-Way Cranberry Sauce (page 151), ¼ cup

Butternut Squash Soufflé (page 133), ½ cup

Pumpkin Mousse with
Gingersnap Topping (page 190), 1 serving

Calories 410
Carbs 38 grams
Fiber 7 grams
Fat 12 grams
Protein 39 grams

Diabetic exchange = 2 Carbohydrates, 5 Very Lean Meat
WW point comparison = 8 points

Compare to:

Turkey meat, white and dark, 4 ounces

Cranberry sauce, ¼ cup

Candied sweet potatoes, ½ cup

Pumpkin pie, 1 slice

Calories 920
Carbs 100 grams
Fiber 5 grams
Fat 40 grams
Protein 39 grams

Diabetic exchange = 5½ Carbohydrate, 5 Lean Meat, 5 Fat
WW point comparison = 20 points

Save: 510 calories, 62 grams carbs, 28 grams fat, and 12 points

Gain: 2 grams fiber

Nutritional Analysis
of the Recipes

COMPLETE NUTRITIONAL INFORMATION IS PROVIDED FOR EACH RECIPE TO help you make wise dietary choices best suited to your needs and health goals. The information was calculated using ESHA Nutrition Food Processor software along with manufacturer's data to ensure accurate information. Here are some additional tips to help make this information even more useful to you.

Portion Sizes

The nutrition and calorie information is only correct if you consume the portion size stated—if you choose to eat more (or less), simply multiply or divide as necessary. I have tried to be realistic in my portions—they are smaller than today's gigantic restaurant portions but not as skimpy as those in many healthy cookbooks!

Diabetic Exchanges

Although many persons with diabetes simply count total carbohydrates rather than using the exchange lists, I have included them because they are still a valuable tool for meal planning. The most current guidelines of the American Diabetes Association were used for the calculations. I hope you will notice just how much healthier these recipes really are. This is especially true when you combine several foods together to make a meal—a good illustration of this is on page 23, "The Fantastic Food with Splenda Difference." If you need help with meal planning, consult a registered dietitian or physician to help to determine the number of exchanges or total nutrients appropriate for you.

Carbohydrate Counts

Most low-carbohydrate diets allow you to subtract fiber from the total carbohydrates, to yield the "net carbs." The grams of carbohydrate provided are the *total* amount of carbohydrates, not net. Simply subtract the grams of fiber to get to the net carbs.

My goal was to create lower-carb foods that taste as great as their traditional (refined carbohydrate) counterparts. Thus, you will find varying carb levels throughout the book. Simply choose the recipes that suit the appropriate carbohydrate level for you at any given time.

Fat

Fat grams are provided, but the percentage of fat in the total calorie count is not. There are several reasons I did not provide this calculation. First, all the recipes are low in fat. Second, the percentage of fat you should eat is based on the total calories for a meal, or a day (or more), not a single food. And last, taking out all of the sugar skews the fat percentage, making it appear higher than normal. Because sugar raises the total calories, but not those from fat, the fat calories divide into a larger number, making the fat percentage appear smaller. (Something food manufacturers who love to add sugar know all too well!) But if you need this figure, multiply the grams of fat by 9 (to get the total calories from fat), and then divide this into the total number of calories and multiply by 100 to reach the percentage of fat of the total calories.

Other Ingredients: As Desired or Optional

Other ingredients, either as desired or optional, are not figured into the total nutritional count. The only exception that *has* been included is the use of powdered sugar as a garnish. But you needn't worry, because the carbohydrate and calories from the small amounts of sugar used for dusting add more in terms of presentation than actual carbohydrates or calories. In fact, these added calories are truly negligible. No suggested ingredients or toppings are included in the nutrition analysis or calorie count unless they are clearly indicated as an integral ingredient in a recipe.

PART II
COOKING AND BAKING TIPS

Slash the Sugar without Sacrificing Taste

THE SUGAR ASSOCIATION (YES, THERE IS AN ASSOCIATION WHOSE SOLE purpose is to promote the consumption of sugar) is quick to tell you of all the wonderful things sugar imparts to food *beyond* acting as a sweetener and flavor enhancer. In fact, sugar contributes to the texture and appearance of many dishes and is often the main reason they taste and look as good as they do. This is why it can be tricky just eliminating sugar and replacing it with any of the substitutes. When it comes to sweetening, Splenda is excellent: it tastes just like sugar and has no aftertaste. Splenda is great for baking, too, because it does not break down under heat. However, Splenda does not caramelize like sugar, nor can it stabilize egg whites or thicken like sugar, but these differences can easily be overcome by applying a bit of kitchen chemistry. In order to understand how I created my recipes with so little sugar and fat, I share the following tips:

Please note: All the recipes have been developed using Splenda Granular. Use Splenda Granular (in the box or bag) except where noted. This product measures cup for cup like sugar and is very easy to use in all recipes and drinks.

- In cold beverages, salad dressings, and where smaller amounts of Splenda are required, Splenda can be used in its packet form. Each packet is the equivalent of 2 teaspoons of sugar. (3 teaspoons = 1 tablespoon)
- To maintain the various properties of browning, texture, and taste that sugar imparts to many dishes, it is necessary to use small amounts of natural sugar in addition to Splenda for the best results (especially in baking). A few carefully selected teaspoons or tablespoons add minimal carbohydrate (compared to *cups* of sugar), yet can make a big difference in the quality and appearance of the food.

- Adding small amounts of molasses or brown sugar to recipes will add color, aid in browning, and contribute a unique flavor. Keep in mind that some baked items will simply be slightly lighter in color than their traditional counterparts.

- Adding cornstarch will help to thicken syrups made with Splenda. If you choose to substitute any of the low-carb thickeners on the market, such as ThickenThin no/starch, follow the instructions on the package. (Please note that the recipes in this book were not tested with those products.)

- When baking with Splenda, additional leavening may be necessary. Splenda's manufacturer recommends that an additional ½ teaspoon of baking soda be added for each cup of Splenda used in a recipe. One drawback to this is that baking soda is high in sodium and can make some foods taste too salty, so try using some additional baking powder as another alternative.

- Splenda does not have the bulk of sugar, so it doesn't give foods the same volume that sugar does. Therefore, the volume, weight, and yield may be smaller than a similar traditional recipe. Adjustments can be made by increasing other ingredients, using a smaller pan size (when there is less batter), and/or changing the portions.

- A tablespoon or two of a liquid sugar, like corn syrup or honey, will help give a more traditional texture to drop cookies. In addition, using a glass or spatula to flatten cookies before baking also helps to make them look like their traditional counterparts.

- Jellies or preserves need to be made using no-sugar pectins. Jams and jellies made without sugar will not be clear and sparkly in appearance. Remember that even a touch of granulated sugar helps clarity.

- Splenda-based frozen desserts freeze very hard. To make "scoopable" again, place in the refrigerator one hour or more before serving to soften a bit.

- Baked goods with Splenda cook faster. Check cakes up to 10 minutes sooner, muffins 5–8 minutes sooner, and cookies 3–5 minutes sooner. Also be sure to adjust the pan size if the batter does not reach the appropriate level in the pan.

- Dust a mere teaspoon or two of powdered sugar or cocoa powder onto desserts through a fine sieve after they are cooled to create a nice appearance. Before or after baking, adding a sprinkle of granulated sugar can add terrific sparkle. (These techniques add less than 1 gram of carbohydrate per serving.)

- Wrap cooled baked goods tightly to keep them from drying out. You may freeze cookies, muffins, quick breads, and plain cakes. Thaw and microwave when you want to bring back that just-baked goodness.

After all is said about the virtues of Splenda (and there are many), I am sad to report that it's impossible for it to work in every type of recipe, especially those that depend on sugar to provide most of the structure or volume (Angel food cake), to caramelize (caramel syrups), or to crystallize (for crackly toppings). I think this is a small price to pay for a product that makes it possible for us to enjoy such a variety of foods without guilt or health risks.

Lowering the Fat—
But Not the Taste

LOWERING THE FAT IN A RECIPE IS NOTHING SPECIAL, BUT TO DO SO WITHOUT compromising flavor is. No one will eat any food, now matter how healthy it is, if it doesn't taste good. It was my goal to create recipes that will be enjoyed by everyone—you, your family, your friends, and even your kids (mine are my toughest critics). The good news is that I think I've succeeded. Here are some of my favorite ways of lowering fat:

- I have not attempted to strip all the fat out of every recipe, but I have lowered it significantly. Fat is needed for flavor and texture. While there are a few great dishes devoid of fat, a small amount of additional fat makes a tremendous difference in the palatability of most foods.

- Choosing the right type of fat for the job allows you to use less, which is always best. For example, while healthy oils are terrific for some recipes, they don't work like solid fat for baking. This means using a smidge of real butter for flavor, olive or canola oils where liquid oils are appropriate, and a healthy reduced-fat margaine (no less than 70 percent fat) for baking to lower saturated fat and cholesterol. (For more information, see the ingredients section.)

- Broths, vegetable and fruit juices, reduced-fat margarine or mayonnaise, and low-fat dairy products can all help reduce the quantity of fat used in a recipe. One-half cup of oil, albeit healthy, delivers 960 calories and 112 grams of fat! A stick of butter adds 800 calories and 88 grams of fat (as does just ½ cup of full-fat mayonnaise).

- When choosing a protein source, think lean, and trim any excess fat before cooking. A good rule of thumb is to look for the word "loin" or "round" in the name.

- Whole eggs add body and richness to recipes, and the yolks don't add as much saturated fat and cholesterol as once thought. A yolk contains 5 grams of fat (and the egg white 0 grams), but only one third of the fat is saturated. Furthermore, the yolk contains iron and essential B vitamins. To reduce the fat, it's best to use a whole egg along with additional egg whites instead of multiple whole eggs. See the ingredient section for other substitutions.

- Low-fat dairy products work beautifully. They are richer tasting than their nonfat counterparts and much healthier than the full-fat versions. To further lower the fat, I often mix low-fat products with nonfat products. Rarely do I use only a nonfat product. An exception is nonfat half-and-half. It is a great replacement for regular half-and-half. I also blend it with 1% milk to get the richness of whole milk with only a fraction of the fat. I do not recommed replacing low-fat products when specified with non-fat products as it may diminish quality.

- Fruit purees are especially useful in baking to provide moistness without fat. Their natural sugars also help the baked goods rise and brown. In my experience this works best when the amount of puree replaces no more than one-half of the original fat in a recipe. I also use applesauce for lighter baked goods and prune puree or baby food prunes for darker or denser foods (like chocolate goodies!).

- Recipes that are low in fat need greater amounts of spices and flavorings. Since I think the key to delicious, low-fat food is bold flavor, I am liberal in my use of spices and flavorings. It also helps if they are fresh and of good quality (like real vanilla).

- A good-quality nonstick pan for sautéing will save an enormous amount of fat and will also save a lot of cleanup time!

- A preheated sauté pan needs less oil to cook food. Starting with a cold pan makes food stick (unless you add *lots* of fat).

- Always use a nonstick cooking spray. Make your own by filling a pump or spray bottle or buy a can of a commercially packaged spray. Just be sure to use only a quick spray. A 1¼-second spray delivers only 1 gram of fat. Spraying for 5 seconds gives you a teaspoon of oil (4.3 grams of fat). But a 15-second spray adds a tablespoon of oil (and 14 grams of additional fat)! The recipes in this book were calculated using a 2- or 3-second spray.

Ingredients to Use

I F YOU WANT GREAT-TASTING FOOD, USE THE BEST INGREDIENTS. ALTHOUGH I have allowed for some substitutions in the recipes, following the basic recipe closely will help ensure that the final product will turn out as intended and that the nutritional information I have supplied is accurate. If you get the urge to embellish on any of the recipes, please do so, but be sure you have the basics down first—then adjust away based on your own taste and health preferences!

Here are a few suggestions about ingredients:

Applesauce

Always use unsweetened applesauce. The sweetened varieties contain significant amounts of added sugar.

Buttermilk

Even though the label may not indicate it, buttermilk is naturally low in fat. Buttermilk is a great low-fat ingredient in dressings, frozen treats, and baked goods, where it aids in tenderizing (this is especially important when the fat and sugar in a recipe are low). Buttermilk can be frozen in usable portions or you can substitute sour milk for fresh buttermilk. To make sour milk, add 1 tablespoon of vinegar or lemon juice to a 1-cup measuring cup. Add 1% milk to fill the cup. Let stand for 3 minutes before using.

Cocoa Powder

Dutch-processed cocoa powder is cocoa powder that has had some of the natural acidity of cocoa neutralized. It brings a darker, smoother cocoa flavor to recipes, especially those that are low in sugar. I use Hershey's European, found in the baking aisle, but any brand is fine.

Cottage Cheese

I love cottage cheese. It's low in carbs, calories, and fat and provides good protein. I use 2% or low-fat cottage cheese in my recipes, but my trick is to *completely* cream it before using. This means it looks as smooth as sour cream, with no remaining curds, after I run it through the food processor or blender.

Cream Cheese

I use Philadelphia brand light cream cheese sold in a tub. You can also substitute Neufchatel cheese with good results, but it is higher in calories and fat. I also recommend Philadelphia nonfat cream cheese sold in an 8-ounce block. I also combine nonfat and low-fat cream cheeses. This technique lowers the fat content yet maintains good flavor. Full-fat cream cheese will significantly increase the calories and fat in a recipe.

Eggs

Pasteurized eggs ensure complete safety from the risk of salmonella poisoning that is always a threat when eating uncooked eggs. Pasteurized eggs can be found as egg substitutes in a carton or as in-the-shell brands like Davidson's. Also, ¼ cup of egg substitute equals 1 large egg or 2 whites. However, I have found that using real eggs produces a better flavor and texture in baking.

Flavorings

Using real vanilla extract and good-quality spices makes a difference in any recipe. Check your spice jars. If you can't smell what's in them when you open the container, they are too old and should be replaced.

Filo Dough

Filo dough offers a lower-fat, lower-carb alternative to traditional piecrusts. You can find it in the freezer section of most food markets. Thawing it slowly, as directed on the package, and covering it with a damp towel while using will keep it from cracking.

Flours

I use many types of flour throughout the book—all-purpose, cake, and whole wheat. Each produces a different result, and substitutions will affect outcomes. Cake flour has less protein and produces a lighter, more tender crumb when used. All-purpose is standard and works best for most baking applications, whereas whole wheat offers more fiber and a heavier, nuttier taste. You may also try using whole wheat pastry flour (which adds fiber but is less heavy) and soy flour (which offers more protein and less carb), but I recommend you do so for no more than one-quarter of the flour with soy and one-half with wheat pastry.

Hoisin

Hoisin is a key ingredient in many Chinese barbeque sauces and stir-fry dishes. It is a thick paste made from soybeans, garlic, sugar, and spices. Small amounts can add great flavor, and there really is no substitute. Look for it in the supermarket in the Asian section.

Margarine and Butter

You may substitute your own favorite brand. The margarine I use is Land O Lakes 70 percent vegetable oil/buttermilk blend stick margarine. The water content of margarines that are less than 70 percent by weight is too high for proper baking. Tub margarines are in this category, as is light butter. Use them only if specified. Also, the total amount of saturated fat and trans fat in the margarine I use is less than 4 grams per tablespoon (and I minimize its use). If you prefer to use butter (with 7 grams of sat fat per tablespoon but no trans fat), the recipes will be higher in fat, saturated fat and calories.

Milk

I have specified low-fat (1%) milk. At 20 percent fat, 1% milk is richer tasting than skim, without the fat of 2% or whole milk. Skim milk can be used, but the recipes will taste and look better with 1%.

Nonfat Half-and-Half

Nonfat or fat-free half-and-half has the creamy richness of half-and-half without the fat. Land O Lakes is the brand I use. You can substitute regular half-and-half in the recipes, but the grams of fat and the calories will be higher. Do not substitute nonfat milk.

Oatmeal

Because oatmeal contains fiber and digests slowly, it does not raise blood glucose as refined flours do. In the recipes I specify old-fashioned oats, which come in regular and quick-cooking varieties. I prefer the regular, larger, uncut oats, especially for toppings, but either will work with the recipes. Do not use instant oatmeal.

Oils

Many different types of oils are used in the recipes and each offers its own taste (or lack of it). Flavorless, monounsaturated canola oil is used for baking, and olive and sesame oils for cooking. When just olive oil is specified, it means it is not necessary to use virgin or extra-virgin varieties. If extra virgin is specified, it means the taste difference is worth the increased cost of the oil. Sesame oil (made from sesame seeds) is a healthful oil with a pronounced nutty taste. Small amounts make a big flavor impact, and the recipes that use it will not be the same without it—there are no substitutes for sesame oil.

Protein Powder

Protein powder is a great way to add protein to recipes without fat or sugar. It is found most commonly in two varieties: the designer-brand packaged in cans and sold at most markets and the yellowish powder found in bags or bins in the health food store. The canned variety works best in drinks and smoothies, while the bagged version works better in baking (it's more like flour). Either way, look for a powder from soy or whey that provides pure protein (usually 25 grams per 2 tablespoons), without any fillers or sugar.

Nonstick Cooking Sprays

I use unflavored vegetable oil sprays made from canola oil, such as regular Pam. Be sure not to use an olive oil or other flavored spray for baking, because the flavor is too strong.

Nonstick Baking Spray

Nonstick baking spray, such as Baker's Joy, contains a small amount of flour in the spray, along with vegetable oil. It makes greasing *and* flouring pans for baking a snap.

Zests

Many recipes call for grated lemon, lime, and orange zests (peels). They add terrific flavor and can be added whenever you see fit. Simply grate the brightly colored outer layer off of the whole fruit (avoiding the bitter white part). Use a box or sharp flat grater that has small holes to make a finely grated, *but not mushy*, zest. If the grated zest does not look finely minced, use a knife to finish it off before adding to the recipe.

Prune Puree

For convenience, baby-food prunes are specified in most of the recipes. They can be pure prunes or a prune with apples blend. I also like to keep on hand a product called Sunsweet Lighter Bake, found in the baking aisle of most stores. It is a dark pureed prune and apple blend. You can also puree 1¼ cups pitted prunes with 6 tablespoons of hot water until smooth to make your own puree. This will make one cup and will keep in the refrigerator for 1–2 months. One tablespoon of puree replaces 2 tablespoons of fat in recipes.

Splenda

Splenda can be found in most grocery stores stocked right next to the sugar, or you can order it directly from www.splenda.com. Splenda is available in Splenda Granular, sold in boxes or large bags, and Splenda packets. I use the Splenda Granular in all the recipes. It measures equivalent to sugar, and provides some bulk for baking. If you choose to substitute packets for beverages or dressings, each packet is the equivalent of 2 teaspoons (thus 3 packets = 2 tablespoons).

Whipped Topping

Light whipped topping is found in tubs in the freezer section of supermarkets; be sure to thaw it before using. The nonfat version is not recommended, because it doesn't taste as good and has a higher sugar content than the light does.

Yogurt

Plain non-fat yogurt may be substituted for low-fat. Otherwise, use only the type of yogurt specified. If regular low-fat yogurt is specified, do not substitute "light" yogurt or artificially sweetened yogurts. The sweetness does not always hold up in baking.

PART III
THE RECIPES

Delicious Drinks

YUM . . . THESE BEVERAGES ARE AMONG MY ALL—TIME FAVORITES! Because, while I love sweet beverages of all kinds, I don't love the sugar and fat they are often full of.

The truth is, sweet beverages taste so good that it's easy to overlook what's in them—but this can be a weighty mistake. In fact, scientific studies have shown that while the calories from liquid beverages really add up, they just don't fill you up like solid food. It means that a 300-calorie coffeehouse favorite or 500-calorie "health" smoothie can easily become "extras" on your scale. That's why I am happy to start this book with lots of ways to indulge your sweet tooth with beverages that do not contain sugar or unwanted calories. You will find everything from cook summer sippers like Citrus Splash and kid-pleasing Hawaiian Fruit Punch to a nutritious Strawberry Almond Smoothie in this section. You'll also find some great coffeehouse favorites, like Indian Chai Tea and Café Orange that will be as easy on your waist as they are on your wallet!

For your holiday gatherings, I have included Old-Fashioned Eggnog and Apple Spiced Tea. You also learn how to make beverage mixes, including Homemade Café Mocha Mix.

Best of all you can relax and enjoy all of these beverages guilt-free—as they are just as sweet and tantalizing as their sugar-laden counterparts. And what could be sweeter than that?

DELICIOUS DRINKS

Strawberry Lemonade

Citrus Splash

Hawaiian Fruit Punch

Chocolate Frostie

Orange Creamsicle Frappe

Strawberry Almond Soy Smoothie

Chocolate Banana Peanut Butter High Protein Shake

Indian Chai Tea

Hot Vanilla Steamer

Café Orange

Apple Spiced Tea

Old-Fashioned Eggnog

Rich, Instant Eggnog for One

Homemade Chai Spice Mix

Homemade Café Mocha Mix

Homemade Hot Chocolate Mix

STRAWBERRY LEMONADE

Pretty in pink—here strawberries turn ordinary lemonade into delicious "pink lemonade." I like the extra fresh taste of the strawberry puree in the lemonade, but you may strain out the pulp if you prefer a clear, crisp pink lemonade— either way it's delicious.

1½ cups strawberries, fresh halved (or frozen, slightly thawed)	⅔ cup Splenda Granular
	3 cups cold water
	2 teaspoons lemon zest
1 cup lemon juice (about 4 medium lemons)	

1. Place strawberries in a food processor or blender; process until smooth and pour into a large pitcher.
2. Add lemon juice to pitcher. Stir in Splenda and water.
3. Strain out strawberry pulp if desired. Add lemon zest.
4. Serve in tall 12-ounce glasses filled with ice.

Serves Four

PER SERVING

Calories 50
Carbohydrate 12 grams
Protein 1 gram

Fat 0 grams (saturated)
Fiber 2 grams
Sodium 0 milligrams

Diabetic exchange = 1 Fruit
WW point comparison = 1 point

 You save over 30 grams of carbohydrate and 100 calories a glass by eliminating the granulated sugar from this lemonade!

CITRUS SPLASH

This refreshing drink is a great breakfast or afternoon sipper, especially if you make it with fresh juices. Lighter and a bit more tart than lemonade, it's the perfect beverage for a hot summer's day. Try it with a twist of lime.

⅔ cup orange juice
½ cup lime juice (about 3 limes)
½ cup lemon juice (about 2 lemons)

6 tablespoons Splenda Granular (or 9 Splenda packets)
2⅓ cups club soda or seltzer water (lime or lemon sparkling water is also nice)

1. Combine juices, Splenda, and club soda in a large pitcher. Stir.
2. Serve immediately over ice in tall 12-ounce glasses.

Serves Four

PER SERVING

Calories 45
Carbohydrate 12 grams
Protein 1 gram

Fat 0 grams (saturated)
Fiber 0 grams
Sodium 0 milligrams

Diabetic exchange = 1 Fruit
WW point comparison =1 point

For a party, measure juices and Splenda into a punch or other pretty large bowl. Just before serving add the ice and club soda. For a garnish, float thin slices of lime, lemon, and oranges on top.

HAWAIIAN FRUIT PUNCH

This recipe is kid tested and mother approved. My boys love that it tastes just like the high-sugar stuff, and I love that it's made without any added sugars. Better yet, a glass delivers almost a day's worth of vitamin C.

2	cups light cranberry juice (like Ocean Spray Lightstyle)	2	tablespoons Splenda Granular (or 3 Splenda packets)
1	cup orange juice	1	cup water
½	cup pineapple juice		

1. Mix all ingredients in a large pitcher. Stir.
2. Serve in 8-oounce glasses filled with ice.

Serves Six

PER SERVING

Calories 45
Carbohydrate 11 grams
Protein 1 gram

Fat 0 grams (0 saturated)
Fiber 0 grams
Sodium 0 milligrams

Diabetic exchange = 1 Fruit
WW point pomparison = 1 point

CHOCOLATE FROSTIE

My son Stephen is the chocolate lover in our family. He loved the Deep Dark Hot Chocolate in Unbelievable Desserts with Splenda *and he's hooked on this. According to him, it's just as good as the ones from the fast-food outlets—only this one can be enjoyed right at home!*

1   individual serving packet Splenda-sweetened sugar-free hot chocolate mix (Swiss Miss)
½   cup 1% milk
1   tablespoon Splenda Granular (or 2 Splenda packets)

2   teaspoons cocoa powder
½   cup sugar-free low-carb vanilla ice cream
½   cup crushed ice

1. Place hot chocolate mix, milk, Splenda, and cocoa in a blender. Blend to mix.
2. Add vanilla ice cream and ice and blend until thick and frosty.

Serves One

PER SERVING

Calories 200
Carbohydrate 24 grams
Protein 13 grams

Fat 5 grams (3.5 saturated)
Fiber 4 grams
Sodium 220 milligrams

Diabetic exchange = ½ Milk, 1 Starch
WW point pomparison = 4 points

 A medium Frosty from Wendy's contains 440 calories, 11 grams of fat, and 73 grams of carbohydrate!

ORANGE CREAMSICLE FRAPPE

As a kid I loved the frothy orange drink called an Orange Julius. This has that same delicious sweet orange/vanilla taste I remember so well. With less sugar and more fun than a cup of regular orange juice, this is sure to please.

¾ cup orange juice
¾ cup 1% milk
¼ cup Splenda Granular
    (or 6 Splenda packets)

¼ cup egg substitute
    (Like Egg Beaters)
¾ teaspoon vanilla
1   cup crushed ice
    (or 5–6 cubes)

1. Place all ingredients except ice in a blender and pulse to blend.
2. Add ice and blend until ice is completely incorporated and drink is frothy.
3. Serve immediately in 8-ounce glasses.

Serves Two

PER SERVING

Calories 110
Carbohydrate 19 grams
Protein 7 grams

Fat 1 gram (0.5 saturated)
Fiber 0 grams
Sodium 100 milligrams

Diabetic exchange = ½ Low-fat Milk, ½ Fruit
WW point comparison = 2 points

The egg gives this drink a protein boost and makes it frothy.

STRAWBERRY ALMOND SOY SMOOTHIE

Let's face it, tofu does not have a very good reputation as a tasty food—good for you, yes, but yummy, no. This shake will change your mind. I've added the delicious combination of strawberries and almond to make one very creamy, very tasty smoothie. (You may actually forget it's good for you.)

1 cup 1% milk	¼ cup Splenda Granular (or 6 Splenda packets)
¾ cup strawberries, fresh, quartered (or frozen, partially defrosted)	¼ teaspoon almond extract
⅓ cup firm silken tofu	½ cup ice

1. Place all ingredients except ice in a blender and pulse to blend. Add ice and blend until thick and creamy.
2. Serve immediately in 8-ounce glasses.

Serves Two

PER SERVING

Calories 110

Carbohydrate 14 grams

Protein 7 grams

Fat 3 grams (1 saturated)

Fiber 1 gram

Sodium 65 milligrams

Diabetic exchange = ½ Low-fat milk, ½ Fruit

WW point comparison = 2 points

Soy is a great source of protein and a healthy addition to any diet. Soy can help lower cholesterol and may also decrease the risk of osteoporosis, heart disease, and some cancers.

CHOCOLATE BANANA PEANUT BUTTER HIGH-PROTEIN SHAKE

The name says it all for this rich, thick, creamy, fill-you-up type of drink. Drink alone as a minimeal or combine this drink with a piece of light whole-wheat toast for a satisfying and nutritious breakfast.

1 banana, peeled, cut in half and frozen	2 teaspoons cocoa powder
1 cup cold 1% milk	2 tablespoons protein powder
2 tablespoons peanut butter	½ cup crushed ice
3 tablespoons Splenda Granular (or 4 Splenda packets)	

1. Place all the ingredients in a blender and blend until thick and smooth.
2. Serve in 8-ounce glasses.

Serves Two

PER SERVING

Calories 250

Carbohydrate 26 grams

Protein 17 grams

Fat 9 grams (3 saturated)

Fiber 3 grams

Sodium 200 milligrams

Diabetic exchange = ½ Low-fat Milk, 1 Fruit, 2 Medium-fat Meat
WW point comparison = 5 points

Eating peanut butter is back in style! Although it's dense in both calories and fat, the fat is monounsaturated, which means it's good for you. So eat up—just not too much.

INDIAN CHAI TEA

Legend has it that a chef in India created this tea for a king. The chef wanted a tea with a luxurious fragrance and so scented it with cloves, cardamom, and nutmeg. Today you simply need to travel to your nearest tea- or coffeehouse to find this sweet and spicy favorite, or you can make this version, which has the same great taste with a fraction of the sugar and calories.

2 cups water	3 tea bags, Darjeeling or black tea
1/4 teaspoon ground cinnamon	1/2 teaspoon vanilla
1/4 teaspoon ground cloves	1/4 cup Splenda
1/4 teaspoon powdered ginger	1 tablespoon honey
1/4 teaspoon ground cardamom	1 cup 1% milk
1/8 teaspoon ground nutmeg	

1. Bring water to a boil with the spices in a small saucepan. Add the tea bags and let steep 2–3 minutes.
2. Remove tea bags and stir in vanilla, Splenda and honey. Strain tea.
3. To serve, measure ⅔ cup tea mixture and ⅓ cup milk into mug and microwave 1 minute or heat tea and milk together in a small saucepan.

Serves Three

PER SERVING

Calories 60
Carbohydrate 12 grams
Protein 3 grams

Fat 1 gram (.5 saturated)
Fiber 0 grams
Sodium 40 milligrams

Diabetic exchange = 1 Carbohydrate
WW point comparison = 1 point

TIP — Feel free to adjust this recipe to your own taste. It is very sweet, just like the most popular versions. If you like yours less sweet, simply use less honey or Splenda. During the holidays I add a touch more nutmeg, and in the summer I like it over ice.

HOT VANILLA STEAMER

My youngest son requests this luscious drink every day! I don't blame him; it's delicious and wonderfully soothing. In fact, it is the perfect bedtime treat.

1 cup minus 2 tablespoons 1% milk	1 tablespoon Splenda Granular (or 2 Splenda packets)
2 tablespoons fat-free half-and-half	½ teaspoon vanilla

1. Place milk and half-and-half in a microwavable 8-ounce mug. Stir in Splenda.
2. Microwave on high for 1½ minutes (until hot, not boiling). Remove from microwave and stir in vanilla.

Serves One

PER SERVING

Calories 120
Carbohydrate 16 grams
Protein 8 grams

Fat 2 grams (1 saturated)
Fiber 0 grams
Sodium 80 milligrams

Diabetic exchange = 1 Low-fat Milk
WW point comparison = 2 points

Fat-free half-and-half is the key to making this drink rich and creamy.

CAFÉ ORANGE

I am not usually a fan of flavored coffees, nor do I like my coffee sweet—but I do love orange zest. In this unique recipe, orange zest is placed directly into coffee grounds and Splenda into the coffeepot before brewing. The result is positively addictive. This is a wonderful coffee to serve with dessert—or for dessert. Simply add your favorite creamer, steamed milk, or light whipped topping.

6   tablespoons ground coffee (NOTE: Standard coffee scoops often measure 2 tablespoons)

1   small orange

3   tablespoons Splenda Granular (or 4 Splenda packets)

2   teaspoons honey (optional)

4   cups water

1. Place coffee in filter. Grate peel of orange into grounds.
2. Measure Splenda and honey into coffee pot. Brew coffee as directed on coffee machine. Add milk or creamer to hot coffee as desired.

Serves Four

PER SERVING (WITH HONEY)

Calories 20
Carbohydrate 5 grams
Protein 0 grams

Fat 0 grams (0 saturated)
Fiber 0 grams
Sodium 0 milligrams

Diabetic exchange = one serving free food
WW point comparison = 0 points

APPLE SPICED TEA

Hot spiced cider can really warm you up on a chilly day. This low-sugar version uses apple tea bags to significantly reduce the carbohydrate content of this seasonal favorite.

3	cups boiling water	1/3	cup Splenda Granular
3	apple (or apple cinnamon) tea bags	1/4	teaspoon allspice
1	cup apple cider	2	cinnamon sticks
1	teaspoon lemon juice	4	1/2 orange slices

1. Measure water into a medium pot. Bring to a boil; turn off heat and add tea bags. Let steep 3 minutes. Discard tea bags.
2. Add juices, Splenda, allspice, cinnamon sticks, and orange slices. Turn on heat and bring back to a simmer (do not boil), and serve in 8-ounce mugs.

Serves Four

PER SERVING

Calories 35
Carbohydrate 9 grams
Protein 0 grams

Fat 0 grams (0 saturated)
Fiber 0 grams
Sodium 0 milligrams

Diabetic exchange = 1/2 Fruit
WW Point comparison = 1 point

Keep tea hot in a Crock-Pot. Its wonderful aroma will welcome your guests.

OLD-FASHIONED EGGNOG

This recipe was a big hit during the holidays and got "two thumbs up" from everyone who drank it. Although you can buy low-fat eggnogs, I have yet to see one that is also low in sugar. In fact, the light or low-fat versions usually contain more sugar than regular. Once made, this keeps very well for up to a week in the refrigerator.

3 cups 1% milk, divided	3 large eggs, well beaten
1½ cups fat-free half-and-half	⅔ cup Splenda Granular
1 tablespoon + 1 teaspoon cornstarch	2 teaspoons vanilla
	½ teaspoon nutmeg

1. In a large saucepan, thoroughly whisk together 1 cup of the 1% milk and next 4 ingredients. Place on stove and cook over low heat, stirring constantly, until mixture is thick enough to coat the back of a spoon. Remove from heat.
2. Stir in vanilla and nutmeg. Stir in remaining milk and cool.
3. Chill and store in refrigerator until served.

VARIATION: For a spiked version, substitute ½ to 1 cup brandy or rum for equal amount of milk.

Serves Eight

PER SERVING

Calories 100
Carbohydrate 11 grams
Protein 6 grams

Fat 3 grams (1.5 saturated)
Fiber 0 grams
Sodium 80 milligrams

Diabetic exchange = 1 Low-fat Milk
WW point comparison = 2 points

 Watch out for those traditional eggnogs—they can contain up to 30 grams of fat and 40 grams of carbohydrate in a mere ½ cup!

RICH, INSTANT EGGNOG FOR ONE

A perfect minimeal replacement that is very quick and very easy. It is also rich, filling, and high in protein and nutrients. What it lacks is the sugar, fat, and the high price tag of many brand-name meal-replacement drinks. Try a hot mug for breakfast.

1	large egg	¼	teaspoon nutmeg
1	cup 1% milk	1	teaspoon vanilla
2	tablespoons Splenda Granular		

1. Place egg in a large microwavable mug and beat well. Add milk, Splenda, and nutmeg and whisk thoroughly (until egg is completely beaten in).
2. Heat in the microwave for 1 minute. Stir. Heat for 30 more seconds or until hot and slightly thickened. *Do not boil*. Remove from microwave, stir in vanilla, and enjoy.

Serves One

PER SERVING

Calories 180

Carbohydrate 13 grams

Protein 15 grams

Fat 7 grams (3 saturated)

Fiber 0 grams

Sodium 80 milligrams

Diabetic exchange = 1 Low-fat Milk, 1 Medium-fat Meat

WW point comparison = 4 points

The egg in this nog is thoroughly cooked, therefore it is not necessary to use pasteurized eggs.

HOMEMADE SPICED CHAI MIX

One popular addition to the flavored drink market is chai tea mixes. Unfortunately, they are very high in sugar content. This solves that problem. It is easy, economical, and can even be used to make a terrific "gift in a jar." In fact, it is a gift I often make for myself!

¾ cup unsweetened instant ice tea mix

¾ cup Splenda Granular

½ cup non-fat dry milk powder

½ cup non-dairy powdered creamer

1 ½ teaspoons cinnamon

1 ½ teaspoons powdered ginger

1 teaspoon ground cloves

¾ teaspoon nutmeg

¾ teaspoon ground cardamom

1. Thoroughly mix all ingredients together. Place in a jar or other airtight container.
2. To serve: Stir 3 tablespoons dry mix into 6 ounces very hot water.

Serves Thirteen

PER SERVING

Calories 30
Carbohydrate 7 grams
Protein 2 grams

Fat 1 gram (0 saturated)
Fiber 0 grams
Sodium 0 milligrams

Diabetic exchange = ½ Carbohydrate
WW point comparison = 1 point

Package this mix in a pretty jar to make a lovely and original gift.

HOMEMADE CAFÉ MOCHA MIX

Café Mocha is clearly one of the most popular coffee drinks, and this mix really fits the bill. Not overly sweet, it has a rich coffee flavor blended with a touch of chocolate and a hint of cinnamon. Keep a jar of it handy so you can prepare a cup anytime the mood hits.

⅔ cup Splenda Granular

½ cup instant coffee (regular or decaffeinated)

½ cup nonfat dry milk powder

½ cup nondairy creamer

⅓ cup Dutch-process cocoa powder

¼ teaspoon cinnamon

1. Thoroughly mix all ingredients together. Place into an airtight container.
2. To serve: Stir 3 tablespoons of the dry mix into 6 ounces very hot water.

Serves Fourteen

PER SERVING (3 tablespoons)

Calories 40
Carbohydrate 7 grams
Protein 2 grams

Fat 1 gram (0 saturated)
Fiber 0 grams
Sodium 15 milligrams

Diabetic exchange = ½ Carbohydrate
WW point comparison = 1 point

Cocoa powder contains heart-healthy antioxidants.

HOMEMADE HOT CHOCOLATE MIX

I often recommend low-calorie hot chocolate to chocoholics looking to curb their calories. This is a delicious, inexpensive alternative to individual packets.

I   **cup nonfat dry milk powder**
½   **cup nondairy dry creamer**
⅔   **cup Dutch-process cocoa
       powder**
⅔   **cup Splenda Granular**

1. Thoroughly mix all ingredients together. Place into an airtight container.
2. To serve: Stir 3 tablespoons of the dry mix into 6 ounces very hot water.

Serves Fourteen

PER SERVING (3 tablespoons)

Calories 45   Fat 1.5 grams (0 saturated)
Carbohydrate 9 grams   Fiber I gram
Protein 3 grams   Sodium 30 milligrams

Diabetic exchange = ½ Carbohydrate
WW point comparison = I point

Try adding a few crushed, sugar-free peppermint candies to the mix to create your own peppermint hot chocolate.

Breakfast Treats

HOT CINNAMON ROLLS, FRESH WARM SCONES, TENDER PANCAKES, and sweet French toast . . . Now these are breakfasts treats worth waking up to. Nothing beats the wonderful aroma of a warm breakfast treat, especially if your sweet tooth wakes up as early as you do. After all, it's only natural. When you wake up, your blood sugar is lower because of the many hours that have passed since last night's dinner (or even that late-night snack). This dip signals your brain that it needs some fuel—and brain fuel is carbohydrates, sugar to be exact. And there is no quicker way to get that sugar than to eat it. The problem with a high-sugar breakfast, however, is that this sets you up to look for more sugar, just a couple of hours down the line, starting what can be a vicious cycle of sweet cravings. The standard solution is to reduce the refined carbohydrates in the morning and add more protein.

My solution—rather than relinquishing my sweet tooth—was to create a bakers dozen of incredibly sweet-tasting breakfast treats that are low in sugar (and high in protein whenever possible), which are certain to put a smile on any sweet-lover's face. For the person on the run there are Big, Bad Breakfast Cookies (yes, cookies for breakfast *and* they're nutritious) and Peanut Butter and Oat Breakfast Bars. Quick everyday treats include Quick Cinnamon Rolls and Sweet Cinnamon French Toast. Lazy Sunday mornings call for Fresh Blueberry Scones or an amazing Apple Cinnamon Puffed Pancake. And for entertaining or extra-special mornings, try the comfort of Louise's Baked French Toast or the wholesome goodness of creamy Baked Oatmeal.

Whatever you choose, you're sure to be showered with sweet appreciation.

BREAKFAST TREATS

Peanut Butter and Oat Breakfast Bar

Big, Bad Breakfast Cookie

Fresh Blueberry Scones

Orange Ginger Scones

Quick Cinnamon Rolls

Apple Cinnamon Puffed Pancake

Lemon Cottage Cheese Pancakes

High-Protein Cinnamon Pancakes

Sweet Cinnamon French Toast

Stuffed French Toast

Baked French Toast

Baked Oatmeal

Great Granola

PEANUT BUTTER AND OAT BREAKFAST BAR

Wrapped up and ready-to-go breakfast bars are a popular food convenience. This simple and healthy version not only works for a quick breakfast with a glass of milk, but it also makes a great afternoon snack.

2 cups old-fashioned rolled oats	⅓ cup peanut butter
1½ cups crispy rice cereal (like Rice Krispies)	3 tablespoons margarine, melted
½ cup whole wheat flour	3 tablespoons honey
⅓ cup chopped raisins	2 teaspoons molasses
1 teaspoon cinnamon	1 cup Splenda Granular
¼ teaspoon salt	4 large egg whites
	1 teaspoon vanilla

1. Preheat oven to 350°F. Spray a 9 × 13-inch baking pan with non-stick cooking spray.
2. In a large bowl mix together the first 6 ingredients. Set aside.
3. In a medium bowl stir together remaining ingredients. Pour peanut butter mixture over oats and stir until well mixed.
4. Pat mixture into prepared pan and bake for 15 minutes. Cool and cut into 18 bars.

Serves Eighteen

PER SERVING

Calories 125
Carbohydrate 18 grams
Protein 4 grams

Fat 4 grams (1 saturated)
Fiber 2 grams
Sodium 110 milligrams

Diabetic exchange = 1 Carbohydrate, 1 Fat
WW point comparison = 2 points

Breakfast bar or candy bar? Some "breakfast bars" get up to 33 percent of their calories (32 grams) from sugar and 50 percent (12 grams) from fat, with very little protein and fiber. They may be quick, but they're definitely not healthy.

BIG, BAD BREAKFAST COOKIE

Cookies for breakfast? You bet! I picked up a cereal cookie at the store recently that labeled itself "Breakfast on the run. . . ." After reading the label, I realized you had better literally be on the run in order to burn it off. Even though it showed a picture of the 4-ounce cookie equaling a bowl of cereal and milk, I calculated that it was actually more like four bowls of cereal or four glasses of milk, and it was supposed to serve four people! So, 450 calories, 12 grams of fat, and 76 grams of carbohydrate later, you'd better be running! Instead, try these big, ba-a-a-d cookies that do, in fact, make a wholesome meal on the run—even for breakfast.

1 cup all-purpose flour	¼ cup chopped dried apricots
1 cup whole wheat pastry flour	¼ cup chopped pecans
1½ cups old-fashioned rolled oats	1 2½-ounce jar baby food prunes (or ¼ cup prune puree)
1 cup Splenda Granular	3 tablespoons canola oil
3 tablespoons brown sugar	3 tablespoons water
1½ teaspoons baking soda	3 large egg whites
1 teaspoon baking powder	1 tablespoon molasses
1½ teaspoons cinnamon	2 teaspoons vanilla

1. Preheat the oven to 350°F. Lightly spray a cookie sheet with nonstick cooking spray.
2. In a very large bowl mix together the first 10 ingredients. Set aside.
3. In a medium bowl whisk together remaining 6 ingredients. Pour prune mixture over dry ingredients and mix with a spoon to form a stiff dough. Scoop ¼ cup (using measuring cup or small ice cream scoop) of dough for each cookie onto cookie sheet and pat flat to form 3½- to 4-inch circle.
4. Bake for 12–15 minutes or until bottoms of cookies are dry. Remove from pan and place on wire rack to cool.

(You may wrap, freeze, and thaw individual cookies if desired.)

Serves Thirteen

PER SERVING

Calories 180
Carbohydrate 30 grams
Protein 5 grams

Fat 4.5 grams (0 saturated)
Fiber 3 grams
Sodium 190 milligrams

Diabetic Exchange = 2 Carbohydrate, 1 Fat
WW point comparison = 3 points

 For variety, try different combinations of friuts and nuts. Some suggestions: dried cranberries or cherries and almonds, or raisins and walnuts.

FRESH BLUEBERRY SCONES

Scones are made from sweetened biscuit dough and can vary quite a bit in their richness. Most of them found in bakeries and coffee shops are quite rich and usually oversized, meaning that they contain a high amount of carbohydrates, fat, and calories. Try to use fresh blueberries in this recipe to give these scones their best appearance; frozen berries will color the dough (giving you a "blue" berry scone).

2	cups all-purpose flour	1	cup buttermilk
⅓	cup Splenda Granular	3	tablespoons margarine, melted
2	teaspoons baking powder		
½	teaspoon baking soda	1	large egg
¼	teaspoon salt	½	teaspoon almond extract
1	cup fresh blueberries	2	teaspoons granulated sugar

1. Preheat oven to 425°F. Spray a cookie sheet with nonstick cooking spray.
2. In a large bowl mix together the flour, Splenda, baking powder, baking soda, and salt. Stir in blueberries; set aside.
3. In a small bowl whisk together the buttermilk, margarine, egg, and almond extract. Pour wet mixture over dry ingredients and stir just until dry ingredients are moistened (do not overmix).
4. Drop by heaping spoonfuls (about ¼ cup) onto prepared baking pan, making 13 mounds. Sprinkle scones with granulated sugar. Bake for 12–15 minutes until lightly browned. Transfer to a wire rack to cool slightly before serving.

Serves Thirteen

PER SERVING

Calories 115
Carbohydrate 18 grams
Protein 3 grams

Fat 3 grams (0 saturated)
Fiber 1 gram
Sodium 220 milligrams

Diabetic exchange = 1 Carbohydrate, 1 Fat
WW point comparison = 2 points

If you want big bakery-style scones, use ½ cup batter for each—they will be 230 calories each with 36 grams of carbohydrate (2 Carbs and ½ Fruit) and 6 grams of fat. Still a far cry from a popular coffeehouse favorite with 550 calories and 28 grams of fat!

ORANGE GINGER SCONES

The orange-ginger combination not only makes these taste wonderful, it also gives them a lovely aroma. These triangular-cut scones are terrific served with low-sugar orange marmalade.

2 cups all-purpose flour	3 tablespoons margarine, cold
1/4 cup Splenda Granular	3/4 cup buttermilk
2 teaspoons baking powder	1 large egg
1/2 teaspoon baking soda	1 tablespoon orange zest
1/4 teaspoon salt	1 tablespoon 1% milk
3/4 teaspoon ginger	1 teaspoon granulated sugar
1/2 teaspoon allspice	

1. Preheat oven to 400°F. Spray a cookie sheet with nonstick cooking spray.
2. In a large bowl mix together the flour, Splenda, baking powder, baking soda, salt, ginger, and allspice. Using your fingertips, two knives, or a pastry blender, cut margarine into flour mixture until crumbly; set aside.
3. In a small bowl whisk together buttermilk, egg, and zest. Pour over dry ingredients and stir just until dry ingredients are moistened.
4. Coat your hands with flour and place dough onto lightly floured surface. Knead gently once or twice to pull dough together and pat into an 8-inch round. Using a sharp knife, cut into 10 equal wedges and transfer to baking sheet.
5. Brush wedges with milk and sprinkle with sugar. Bake for 12–15 minutes or until lightly browned. Transfer to a wire rack to cool slightly before serving.

Serves Ten

PER SERVING

Calories 140
Carbohydrate 22 grams
Protein 4 grams

Fat 4 grams (1 saturated)
Fiber 1 gram
Sodium 260 milligrams

Diabetic exchange = 1 1/2 Carbohydrate, 1 Fat
WW point comparison = 3 points

Southern cooks have known all along that buttermilk makes biscuits nice and tender. The acid gives buttermilk its tenderizing properties and works just as well in the sweetened biscuits we call scones.

QUICK CINNAMON ROLLS

You won't have a problem getting the family to the breakfast table when you bake a pan full of these fragrant cinnamon rolls. Because you start with store-bought ready-made dough, they are a quick and easy breakfast treat.

1 11-ounce tube of Pillsbury French loaf bread dough (refrigerated)	1½ tablespoons dark brown sugar
	2 teaspoons cinnamon
2 teaspoons flour	3 tablespoons margarine, softened
⅓ cup Splenda Granular	2 teaspoons powdered sugar

1. Preheat oven to 375°F. Spray 9-inch round pan with nonstick cooking spray.
2. Open tube of bread loaf. Set on work surface dusted with flour. Look for seam and unroll loaf. Using rolling pin, shape into a 15 × 10-inch rectangle.
3. In a small bowl combine Splenda, brown sugar, and cinnamon. Spread margarine onto dough and evenly coat with cinnamon/sugar mixture. Using hands, pat sugar mixture into margarine. Roll up jelly roll–style from the short (10-inch) side of dough. Wet the far edge of dough with water to seal roll. Turn dough onto seam and, using a sharp knife, cut into 10 1-inch slices. Place slices cut-side up in prepared pan and pat down slightly.
4. Bake for 18–20 minutes or until nicely browned. Dust rolls with powdered sugar and serve. (Best while warm—reheat any leftover rolls briefly in microwave.)

Serves Ten

PER SERVING

Calories 105
Carbohydrate 17 grams
Protein 3 grams

Fat 3.5 grams (1 saturated)
Fiber 0 grams
Sodium 260 milligrams

Diabetic exchange = 1 Carbohydrate, ½ Fat
WW point comparison = 2 points

APPLE CINNAMON PUFFED PANCAKE

This pretty cinnamon-scented pancake "puff" is so delicious and sweet on its own, it needs only a light dusting of powdered sugar to finish it off (no butter or syrup required). I serve it up with lean ham or sausage and a few slices of fresh orange.

2 teaspoons butter	½ cup flour
2 teaspoons brown sugar	¼ cup Splenda
1 small apple, peeled, cored, and diced fine	¾ teaspoon cinnamon
⅔ cup 1% milk	½ teaspoon vanilla
2 large eggs + 1 egg white	1 teaspoon powdered sugar, optional

1. Preheat oven to 425°F. Melt butter in a 10-inch ovenproof skillet. Add brown sugar and diced apple and sauté for 3–4 minutes to soften apple.
2. In a medium bowl whisk together milk, eggs, flour, Splenda, cinnamon, and vanilla until smooth. Pour into the hot pan over the cooked apple and immediately place in hot oven. Bake for 15 minutes at 425°, lower oven to 375°, and bake an additional 10–15 minutes or until pancake has risen and edges are curled up and browned.
3. Dust with powdered sugar if desired and serve.

Serves Three

PER SERVING

Calories 210
Carbohydrate 26 grams
Protein 9 grams

Fat 7 grams (2.5 saturated)
Fiber 2 grams
Sodium 120 milligrams

Diabetic exchange = 1½ Carbohydrate, 1 Fat
WW point comparison = 4 points

Just 2 tablespoons of syrup has as much carbohydrate as an entire serving of this flavorful sweetened pancake.

LEMON COTTAGE CHEESE PANCAKES

These sweet lemon-flavored pancakes use less flour than traditional pancakes and do not require additional butter or syrup, although a sprinkling of fresh raspberries is very nice. The cottage cheese gives them a soft, puddinglike texture.

2 **large eggs**	1 **tablespoon lemon juice**
¾ **cup low-fat cottage cheese**	**Zest of one lemon**
½ **cup flour**	½ **teaspoon vanilla**
⅓ **cup Splenda Granular**	3 **teaspoons powdered sugar (optional)**
2 **tablespoons margarine, melted**	

1. In a large bowl beat eggs. Add remaining ingredients (except powdered sugar) and mix until smooth.
2. Heat a large skillet or griddle and coat lightly with oil or cooking spray. When hot, ladle about 3 tablespoons of batter per pancake onto pan. Spread batter evenly to 3-inch diameter. Cook for 1–2 minutes until bottom is brown and firm. Flip pancake and cook until underside is browned. (For firmer pancakes press lightly on pancake after turning.) Place 3 pancakes on a plate and dust with a teaspoon of powdered sugar. Serve plain or with berries.

Serves Three (3 pancakes, including powdered sugar)

PER SERVING

Calories 250	Fat 10 grams (2.5 saturated)
Carbohydrate 21 grams	Fiber 0 grams
Protein 14 grams	Sodium 340 milligrams

Diabetic exchange = 1½ Carbohydrate, 2 Fat
WW point comparison = 5 points

Compare: Three 4-inch frozen pancakes, with a mere teaspoon of butter and a tablespoon of syrup on each, contain 550 calories, 19 grams of fat, and 630 milligrams of sodium. They also give you only 6 grams of protein but a whopping 93 grams of carbohydrate.

HIGH-PROTEIN CINNAMON PANCAKES

I must admit I was pretty skeptical at first of recipes that use protein powder in place of flour. But when an author I really admire used it in her pancakes, I figured it was worth a try. Much to my surprise these cakes cooked up nice and light. Upon running the nutritional analysis, I was even more impressed—15 grams of protein in 2 pancakes, and a reduction of carbohydrate by 50 percent. Wow. They are terrific paired with Apple Cider Butter Syrup (page 266).

½ cup + 2 tablespoons all-purpose flour	1 teaspoon cinnamon
½ cup protein powder	1½ cups buttermilk
¼ cup Splenda Granular	1 tablespoon margarine or butter, melted
1 teaspoon baking powder	2 eggs, lightly beaten

1. In a medium bowl combine the dry ingredients.
2. In a small bowl whisk together the buttermilk, melted margarine, and eggs. Stir into the dry ingredients using a spoon or rubber spatula just until all of the flour in moistened. Do not overmix.
3. Place a griddle or skillet over medium heat. Spray lightly with non-stick cooking spray. Pour ¼ cup batter and spread into 4-inch circle for each pancake. Cook pancake for 3–4 minutes on first side until underside browns. Flip pancake and cook on second side 2–3 minutes. Serve hot with syrup if desired.

Serves Four (two 4-inch pancakes per serving)

PER SERVING

Calories 170
Carbohydrate 18 grams
Protein 15 grams

Fat 5 grams (saturated 1.5)
Fiber 1 gram
Sodium 400 milligrams

Diabetic exchange = 2 Lean Meat, 1 Carbohydrate
WW point comparison = 4 points

I have discovered that the fluffy beige- or yellow-tinged soy-based protein powders found either in bins or bags work better as a substitute for flour than the canned varieties (which I like for drinks) do. I tested these using Bob's Red Mill brand.

SWEET CINNAMON FRENCH TOAST

Traditional French toast recipes are often made with cream and butter. This version cuts down on the fat and calories while retaining all of the flavor! Serve with one of the new Splenda-sweetened sugar-free syrups or your favorite low-sugar jam.

1 large egg + 2 egg whites	½ teaspoon cinnamon
1 cup 1% milk	8 slices cinnamon swirl bread
2 tablespoons Splenda Granular	(I use Pepperidge Farm
¾ teaspoon vanilla	Cinnamon Swirl)

1. Heat griddle or large skillet coated with non-stick cooking spray to medium.
2. Whisk together in a shallow bowl all ingredients except bread. Soak slices of bread one by one into egg mixture until saturated but not falling apart.
3. Place bread into hot skillet and cook until underside is golden brown. Turn and cook until second side is golden brown. Serve immediately.

Serves Four (2 slices each)

PER SERVING

Calories 220
Carbohydrate 32 grams
Protein 11 grams

Fat 7 grams (2 saturated)
Fiber 4 grams
Sodium 300 milligrams

Diabetic exchange = 2 Carbohydrate, 1 Fat
WW point comparison = 4 points

Made with cream, this recipe would contain 30 grams of fat—half of it saturated!

STUFFED FRENCH TOAST

When stuffed with sweet strawberry cream cheese, French toast becomes an extraordinary breakfast. This rich-tasting recipe finished off in the oven serves eight, making it an ideal recipe for a special occasion. Serve with lean ham and fresh strawberries for a beautiful brunch.

FILLING:
- 8 ounces light tub-style cream cheese
- ¼ cup Splenda Granular
- 2 tablespoons low-sugar strawberry (or other fruit) preserves

EGG MIXTURE:
- 2 large eggs + 2 egg whites
- ½ cup nonfat half-and-half
- ½ cup 1% milk
- ¼ cup Splenda Granular
- 2 tablespoons flour
- 2 teaspoons baking powder
- 1 teaspoon vanilla

FRENCH TOAST:
- 16 pieces Italian or French bread (1½ pounds)
- 1 tablespoon powdered sugar (optional)

1. Preheat oven to 400°F. Spray baking sheet with cooking spray. Heat griddle or large skillet coated with nonstick cooking spray to medium.
2. **FILLING:** In a small bowl blend together cream cheese, Splenda, and preserves. Set aside.
3. **EGG MIXTURE:** In a medium bowl whisk together eggs, half-and-half, milk, Splenda, flour, baking powder, and vanilla. Set aside.
4. Spread 2 tablespoons of cream cheese mixture onto half of bread slices. Top each slice with another piece of bread and press together. Soak each sandwich in egg mixture until saturated but not falling apart. Place sandwich in hot skillet and cook until one side is golden brown. Turn and cook until second side is golden brown. Transfer each piece to baking sheet.
5. Baked sautéed slices until puffed up and golden brown, about 5 minutes. Dust powdered sugar over tops and serve immediately.

Serves Eight (with powdered sugar)

PER SERVING

Calories 270
Carbohydrate 39 grams
Protein 12 grams

Fat 7 grams (3 saturated)
Fiber 2 grams
Sodium 600 milligrams

Diabetic exchange = 2½ Carbohydrate, 1½ Lean Meat
WW point comparison = 5 points

BAKED FRENCH TOAST

I'd like to thank Louise Huskins for this recipe. She told me that the idea came to her when a friend had made a similar recipe for Christmas breakfast. Louise refined her recipe with techniques she learned from my first Splenda cookbook. She was so pleased with her results that she sent this recipe to me on Christmas morning! What a great Christmas gift!

4	ounces light tub-style cream cheese	1	cup egg substitute (like Egg Beaters)
4	ounces fat-free tub-style cream cheese	2	large eggs
¾	cup Splenda Granular	3	cups 1% milk
3	tablespoons margarine, softened	1	pound cinnamon raisin, French, or wheat bread (1-inch slices)
2	teaspoons vanilla	2	teaspoons powdered sugar (optional)
1½	teaspoons cinnamon		

1. Spray a 9 × 13-inch baking dish or 2 smaller (9 × 9-inch) baking pans with nonstick cooking spray.
2. In a large bowl beat cream cheeses, Splenda, margarine, vanilla, and cinnamon until smooth. Blend in egg substitute (¼ cup at a time) and then eggs. Add milk and mix well. Soak bread slices in egg mixture and place into prepared pan. Pour remaining batter over slices. Cover and refrigerate for at least an hour and even overnight.
3. Preheat oven to 350°F. Bake for 40–45 minutes until puffed in center and lightly browned. Remove from oven and lightly dust with powdered sugar if desired.

Serves Twelve

PER SERVING

Calories 210
Carbohydrate 24 grams
Protein 11 grams

Fat 7 grams (0 saturated)
Fiber 2 grams
Sodium 320 milligrams

Diabetic exchange = 1 Carbohydrate, ½ Low-fat Milk, 1 Medium-fat Meat
WW point comparison = 4 points

Serving suggestion: Serve with Boysenberry Syrup (page 265) or bottled sugar-free maple syrup and fresh berries. Add Canadian bacon and Café Orange (page 55) or Indian Chai Tea (page 53). Your family and guests are sure to be pleased.

BAKED OATMEAL

OVEN

This is the best oatmeal recipe I know. This is a light soufflé style oatmeal. It is very creamy and will remind you of an oatmeal pudding. The finished dish is so sweet and flavorful that it doesn't require any additional syrup or butter.

OATMEAL:

2 cups old-fashioned oats, uncooked

½ cup Splenda Granular

½ cup raisins

½ teaspoon cinnamon

½ teaspoon salt

2 cups 1% milk

½ cup nonfat half-and-half

½ cup sugar-free maple syrup

4 large egg whites, lightly beaten

2 tablespoons margarine, melted

2 teaspoons vanilla

TOPPING:

1 tablespoon brown sugar

1 tablespoon Splenda Granular

½ teaspoon cinnamon

1. Heat oven to 350°F. Spray 1½-quart soufflé dish with cooking spray.
2. In a large bowl combine the oats, Splenda, raisins, cinnamon, and salt; mix well. In a medium bowl combine milk and remaining liquid ingredients. Add milk mixture to dry ingredients and stir. Pour into baking dish.
3. Bake for 30 minutes. While baking, prepare topping: Combine brown sugar, Splenda, and cinnamon. Sprinkle on topping and bake for additional 15–20 minutes or until center puffs slightly and is firm to the touch.

Serves Eight

PER SERVING

Calories 190
Carbohydrate 24 grams
Protein 8 grams

Fat 4.5 grams (1 saturated)
Fiber 2 grams
Sodium 350 milligrams

Diabetic exchange = 1 Carbohydrate, 1 Fat, ½ Low-fat Milk
WW point comparison = 3 points

Oatmeal is a wonderful source of soluble fiber, which helps to blunt the insulin response and lower the glycemic index of this healthful whole grain.

GREAT GRANOLA

Granola is one of those "health" foods that isn't always so healthy. Depending on how it's made, it can be high in fat and sugar, making it a dense source of both calories and carbohydrates. This reduced-sugar and reduced-fat version is loaded with flavor and makes a great crunchy topping for yogurt or fruit.

3 cups old-fashioned rolled oats	1 cup Splenda Granular
1½ cups puffed wheat cereal	2 tablespoons canola oil
½ cup wheat germ	2 teaspoons molasses
½ cup unsweetened coconut	2 teaspoons vanilla
½ cup sliced almonds	2 large egg whites
2 teaspoons cinnamon	⅓ cup dried cranberries or raisins
¼ teaspoon salt	
6 tablespoons sugar-free syrup	

1. Preheat oven to 250°F.
2. Place oats, cereal, wheat germ, coconut, almonds, cinnamon, and salt in a large bowl.
3. In a small bowl whisk together syrup, Splenda, oil, molasses, vanilla, and egg whites. Pour over cereal mixture and toss. Spread granola onto a baking sheet or jelly roll pan and bake for 30 minutes. Stir and bake additional 30 minutes. Remove from oven and toss in dried cranberries.

Serves Eighteen (⅓ cup)

PER SERVING

Calories 125	Fat 5 grams (1 saturated)
Carbohydrate 16 grams	Fiber 3 grams
Protein 4 grams	Sodium 40 milligrams

Diabetic exchange = 1 Carbohydrate, 1 Fat
WW point comparison = 2 points

Marvelous Muffins, Quick Breads, and Coffee Cakes

I LOVE MUFFINS AND QUICK BREADS. APPARENTLY, I AM NOT ALONE. MORE than ever, muffins, slices of quick breads, and coffee cakes are routine staples not only in bakeries, but also at coffee shops, cafeterias, and even gas stations! Muffins and quick breads make handy, quick, sweet snacks and are easy to make in a variety of scrumptious flavors like pumpkin, lemon, chocolate, and cranberry. What's not so great is the high amount of sugar and fat packed into many recipes and commercially prepared versions of these tasty treats. Believe it or not, it's not uncommon for a single muffin or a piece of coffee cake to contain over 500 calories, 30 grams of fat, and 75 grams of carbohydrate (that's more than many desserts)!

But, thanks to Splenda, I have re-created these sweet treats in all the same great flavors you'll find elsewhere. Not only are these recipes easy to make, but they all freeze well. Simply wrap single servings up tight in plastic wrap, freeze, and then reheat a piece whenever you're in the mood.

If you're a muffin fan, you'll find fresh Banana Bran Muffins, Spicy Pumpkin Muffins, and moist Chocolate Cherry Muffins among my offerings. For the quick bread fan, I have included classic favorites like Lemon Blueberry Bread and Cranberry Orange Tea Bread. Coffee cake lovers can feast on Buttermilk Pecan Crumb Cake and S'more Crumb Cake, which is sure to leave you wanting "some more."

I was very pleased to discover that many of the recipes in this section were the perfect complement to the beverages in the previous section. With that in mind, when you entertain or when you want to treat yourself, consider these winning combinations:

Lemon Blueberry Bread (page 93) and Strawberry Lemonade (page 46)
Banana Bran Muffins (page 84) and Orange Creamsicle Frappe (page 50)
Fresh Carrot Muffins (page 86) and Café Orange (page 55)
Spicy Pumpkin Muffins (page 96) and Indian Chai Tea (page 53)
Buttermilk Pecan Crumb Cake (page 96) and Old-Fashioned Eggnog (page 57)
And for the kids—S'more Crumb Cake (page 98) and Hawaiian Fruit Punch (page 48)

MARVELOUS MUFFINS, QUICK BREADS, AND COFFEE CAKES

Banana Bran Muffins

Chocolate Cherry Muffins

Fresh Carrot Muffins

Lemon Cheese Danish Muffins

Oatmeal Muffins

Spicy Pumpkin Muffins

Cranberry Orange Tea Bread

Lemon Blueberry Bread

Zucchini Walnut Bread

Sour Cream Almond Poppy Seed Loaf

Buttermilk Pecan Crumb Cake

S'more Crumb Cake

BANANA BRAN MUFFINS

These muffins are so wonderfully moist, light, and loaded with fresh banana that you'd never guess that they are so low in fat and so high in fiber.

1 cup mashed banana (about 2 medium bananas)	2 teaspoons molasses
1 cup unsweetened shredded bran cereal (like All-bran)	1 teaspoon vanilla
	1 cup all-purpose flour
¼ cup buttermilk	¼ cup Splenda Granular
2 large egg whites	1 teaspoon baking soda
2 tablespoons canola oil	1 teaspoon baking powder
	½ teaspoon cream of tartar

1. Preheat oven to 400°F. Spray muffin tin with nonstick baking spray.
2. In a medium bowl stir together the first 7 ingredients. Set aside for at least 5 minutes to soften bran.
3. In a large bowl combine flour, Splenda, baking soda, baking powder, and cream of tartar. Stir; make a well and add the liquid mixture, stirring just until blended. Spoon into prepared muffin cups.
4. Bake for 15 minutes or until center springs back when lightly touched. Cool for 5 minutes before removing to a wire rack.

Serves Twelve

PER SERVING

Calories 110
Carbohydrate 19 grams
Protein 3 grams

Fat 3 grams (0 saturated)
Fiber 3 grams
Sodium 220 milligrams

Diabetic exchange = 1 Carbohydrate, ½ Fat
WW point comparison = 2 points

 Do not use bran flakes or powdered unprocessed bran for these muffins.

CHOCOLATE CHERRY MUFFINS

My intention here was to create a muffin reminiscent of a classic Black Forest cake. Although these are muffins, they are wonderfully fudgy and decadent enough to be served as a cupcake.

1½ cups frozen unsweetened dark cherries, partially thawed, cut in half

2 tablespoons Splenda Granular

¾ teaspoon almond extract

¾ cup 1% milk

½ cup unsweetened applesauce

3 tablespoons canola oil

3 tablespoons brown sugar

2 egg whites

1 teaspoon vanilla

1½ cups all-purpose flour

1 cup Splenda Granular

⅓ cup Dutch-process cocoa powder

1½ teaspoons baking powder

½ teaspoon baking soda

2 teaspoons powdered sugar

1. Preheat oven to 375°F. Spray muffin tin with nonstick baking spray.
2. In a small bowl stir together cherries, 2 tablespoons Splenda, and almond extract. Set aside.
3. In a medium bowl whisk together next 6 ingredients. Set aside.
4. In a large bowl combine flour, 1 cup Splenda, cocoa powder, baking powder, and baking soda. Stir; make a well and add liquid mixture, stirring just until blended. Carefully stir in cherries, taking care not to overmix. Spoon into prepared muffin cups.
5. Bake for 18–20 minutes or until center springs back when lightly touched. Cool for 5 minutes before removing to a rack. Dust with powdered sugar.

Serves Twelve

PER SERVING

Calories 145
Carbohydrate 22 grams
Protein 3 grams

Fat 5 grams (0 saturated)
Fiber 1 gram
Sodium 220 milligrams

Diabetic exchange = 1½ Carbohydrate, 1 Fat
WW point comparison = 3 points

Dutch-process cocoa, like Hershey's European brand, is less acidic and therefore less bitter than traditional cocoa powder.

FRESH CARROT MUFFINS

Moist, sweet and spicy—these muffins are terrific. I re-worked this recipe several times to make sure these muffins are every bit as good as the ones I enjoy from the bakery near my home. When all my tasters loved them as much as I do, I knew I had it right.

¾	cup buttermilk	¾	cup all-purpose flour
3	tablespoons canola oil	1	cup Splenda Granular
1	tablespoon molasses	1½	teaspoons baking soda
¼	cup prune puree or 1 jar baby food prunes (2.5 ounces)	1	teaspoon baking powder
		1½	teaspoons cinnamon
1	large egg + 1 egg white	½	teaspoon allspice
1	cup shredded carrots	¼	teaspoon ground cloves
¾	cup whole wheat flour	⅓	cup raisins, chopped

1. Preheat oven to 375°F. Spray muffin tin with nonstick baking spray.
2. In a medium bowl stir together the first 7 ingredients (buttermilk through carrots). Set aside.
3. In a large bowl combine flours, Splenda, baking soda, baking powder, spices, and raisins. Stir; make a well and add the liquid mixture, stirring just until blended. Spoon into prepared muffin cups.
4. Bake for 20 minutes or until center springs back when lightly touched. Cool for 5 minutes before removing to a wire rack.

VARIATION: Substitute chopped nuts for the raisins. (Adds 2 grams of fat and 10 calories but subtracts 3 grams of carbohydrate.)

Serves Twelve

PER SERVING

Calories 130
Carbohydrate 20 grams
Protein 4 grams

Fat 4 grams (0 saturated)
Fiber 3 grams
Sodium 180 milligrams

Diabetic exchange = 1 Carbohydrate, 1 Vegetable, 1 Fat
WW point comparison = 2 points

Try topping these with light cream cheese sweetened with Splenda and/or flavored with orange zest.

LEMON CHEESE DANISH MUFFIN

These delicious muffins combine the things we like best about muffins and Danish. They are light-textured muffins with a spot of cheese Danish filling hidden in the center, and they are crowned with a touch of powdered sugar. They would make a lovely addition to a brunch or luncheon.

FILLING:

4   ounces light tub-style cream cheese

3   tablespoons Splenda Granular

2   teaspoons 1% milk

⅛   teaspoon almond extract

MUFFIN BATTER:

1   large egg

3   tablespoons margarine, melted

¼   cup 1% milk

½   teaspoon vanilla extract

8   ounces regular nonfat lemon yogurt*

2   cups + 2 tablespoons cake flour

¾   cup Splenda Granular

1   teaspoon baking powder

1   teaspoon baking soda

Grated zest of 1 lemon (2 teaspoons)

2   teaspoons powdered sugar (optional)

1. Preheat oven to 400°F. Spray muffin tin with nonstick baking spray.
2. **FILLING:** In a small bowl cream together cream cheese, 3 tablespoons Splenda, milk, and extract. Set aside.
3. **BATTER:** In another small bowl whisk together egg, margarine, milk, vanilla, and yogurt. Set aside.
4. In a large bowl combine flour, ¾ cup Splenda, baking powder, baking soda, and lemon zest. Stir; make a well and add liquid mixture, stirring just until blended.
5. Spoon large tablespoon of batter into each muffin cup (about ½ full), place 2 teaspoons cheese mixture over each, fill cups with remaining muffin batter. Bake for 16–18 minutes or until center springs back when lightly touched. Cool in pans 5 minutes before removing to wire rack. Before serving, dust with powdered sugar.

*Do not use light or sugar-free yogurt. The added sugar in the yogurt enhances the muffin quality and adds only a small amount of carbohydrate per muffin.

Serves Twelve

PER SERVING

Calories 140
Carbohydrate 20 grams
Protein 4 grams

Fat 5 grams (2 saturated)
Fiber 0 grams
Sodium 210 milligrams

Diabetic exchange = 1½ Carbohydrate, 1 Fat
WW point comparison = 3 points

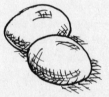

 A wonderful and easy twist is to use low-sugar raspberry jam instead of the cream cheese filling. It adds 1 gram of carbohydrate but lowers the fat to 3.5 total grams and the calories to 130.

OATMEAL MUFFINS

Imagine a bowl of oatmeal with all your favorite toppings rolled into a muffin. Moist, wholesome, and high in fiber, these muffins are a tasty twist on a traditional standby.

MUFFIN BATTER:

- ½ cup 1% milk
- ¼ cup sugar-free syrup (Log Cabin or Carey's)
- ¼ cup unsweetened applesauce
- 3 tablespoons 70% stick margarine, melted (or 2 tablespoons canola oil)
- 2 egg whites
- 1 cup uncooked old fashioned oats (not quick cooking)

- ¾ cup whole wheat flour
- ½ cup all-purpose flour
- ½ cup Splenda Granular
- 1½ teaspoons cinnamon
- 1½ teaspoons baking powder
- ½ teaspoon baking soda

TOPPING:

- 1 tablespoon brown sugar
- 1 tablespoon Splenda Granular
- ½ teaspoon cinnamon

1. Preheat oven to 350°F. Spray muffin tin with nonstick baking spray.
2. **BATTER**: In a small bowl whisk together the first 5 ingredients. Set aside.
3. In a large bowl combine oats, flours, ½ cup Splenda, cinnamon, baking powder, and baking soda. Stir; make a well and add liquid mixture, stirring just until blended. Fill prepared muffin cups ⅔-way full.
4. **TOPPING**: Combine brown sugar, Splenda, and cinnamon. Sprinkle over muffins. Bake for 20 minutes or until center springs back when lightly touched. Cool for 5 minutes before removing to a wire rack.

(These are at their best served the day they are baked.)

Serves Twelve

PER SERVING

Calories 110
Carbohydrate 18 grams
Protein 4 grams

Fat 3 grams (.5 saturated)
Fiber 2 grams
Sodium 130 milligrams

Diabetic exchange = 1 Carbohydrate, ½ Fat
WW point comparison = 2 points

Oats are a great source of soluble fiber and help reduce cholesterol when consumed regularly.

SPICY PUMPKIN MUFFINS

One of my most dog-eared recipes in my dessert book—Unbelievable Desserts with Splenda—was the Pumpkin Pecan Bread. I was asked many times whether it could be baked up as muffins (and it can). I have taken that bread recipe one step further by transforming it into a delectable darker and spicier muffin, which also works as a quick bread. If you're looking for a recipe to serve during the winter holidays, these delicious muffins are a perfect choice.

¾ cup pumpkin puree	2 teaspoons baking powder
1 cup Splenda Granular	½ teaspoon baking soda
6 tablespoons buttermilk	1½ teaspoons cinnamon
3 tablespoons canola oil	1 teaspoon ginger
3 tablespoons molasses	½ teaspoon allspice
1 large egg + 1 large egg white	¼ teaspoon cloves
1½ cups all-purpose flour	¼ teaspoon salt

1. Preheat oven to 375°F. Spray muffin tin with nonstick baking spray.
2. In a medium bowl stir together the first 7 ingredients (pumpkin through eggs). Set aside.
3. In a large bowl combine flour, baking powder, baking soda, spices, and salt. Stir; make a well and add the liquid mixture, stirring just until blended. Spoon into 10 prepared muffin cups.
4. Bake for 20 minutes or until center springs back when lightly touched. Cool in pan for 5 minutes before removing to a wire rack.

Serves Ten

PER SERVING

Calories 150
Carbohydrate 22 grams
Protein 4 grams

Fat 5 grams (0 saturated)
Fiber 1 gram
Sodium 180 milligrams

Diabetic exchange = 1½ Carbohydrate, 1 Fat
WW point comparison = 3 points

CRANBERRY ORANGE TEA BREAD

The classic pairing of orange and cranberries has made this holiday bread a year-round favorite. With its orange glaze and orange-tinted crumb flecked with bright red cranberries, this is a gorgeous loaf for giving and for eating!

LOAF BATTER:

- ½ cup orange juice (or juice from 1 orange + water to make ½ cup)
- ⅓ cup 1% milk
- 3 tablespoons canola oil
- 1 large egg + 1 egg white
- 1 tablespoon orange zest (zest of 1 orange)
- 1 teaspoon vanilla

- 2 cups all-purpose flour
- 1 cup Splenda Granular
- 2 teaspoons baking powder
- ½ teaspoon baking soda
- ¼ teaspoon salt
- 1⅓ cups fresh cranberries, chopped

GLAZE:

- ¼ cup orange juice
- ¼ cup Splenda Granular

1. Preheat oven to 350°F. Coat a 9 × 5-inch* loaf pan with nonstick baking spray.
2. In a medium bowl stir together the first 7 ingredients (juice through vanilla). Set aside.
3. In a large bowl combine flour, Splenda, baking powder, baking soda, salt, and cranberries. Stir; make a well and add the liquid mixture, stirring just until blended. Spoon into prepared pan.
4. Bake for 50 minutes or until center springs back when lightly touched.
5. GLAZE: While bread is baking, combine orange juice and Splenda in a small saucepan. Place on medium heat and reduce by one half. Brush glaze onto warm loaf immediately after removing from oven. Cool in pan on wire rack for 15 minutes before removing from pan.

*VARIATION: Make 2–3 small loaves—fill mini-loaf pans ⅔ full and bake for 30–35 minutes.

Serves Twelve

PER SERVING

Calories 140

Fat 4 grams (0 saturated)

Carbohydrate 22 grams

Fiber 1 gram

Protein 3 grams

Sodium 170 milligrams

Diabetic exchange = 1½ Carbohydrate, 1 Fat

WW point comparison = 3 points

 Cranberries freeze well. Just buy an extra bag or two when they're on sale at Thanksgiving and pop them into the freezer. You'll have them on hand to make this bread any time of year.

LEMON BLUEBERRY BREAD

This blueberry-studded, lemon quick bread is one of my favorites. It's simple to make, beautiful to look at, and incredibly delicious. It's great with a cup of coffee or tea and rich enough to serve as dessert when topped with a dollop of light whipped topping.

⅔ cup 1% milk	1 cup Splenda Granular
1 large egg	2 cups all-purpose flour
1 teaspoon vanilla	2 teaspoons baking powder
4 tablespoons margarine, melted	½ teaspoon baking soda
6 ounces low-fat lemon yogurt (I use Yoplait)	1 cup fresh blueberries (½ pint)
Grated zest of one lemon	1 teaspoon granulated sugar

1. Preheat oven to 350°F. Coat a 9 × 5-inch loaf pan with nonstick baking spray.
2. In a medium bowl whisk together milk, egg, vanilla, margarine, yogurt, zest, and Splenda. Set aside.
3. In a large bowl combine flour, baking powder, baking soda, and blueberries. Stir; make a well in the center and pour in wet ingredients. Mix gently with a spoon until batter is just smooth. Spoon batter into prepared pan. Smooth and sprinkle with sugar.
4. Bake for 45 minutes or until toothpick inserted into center comes out clean.
5. Cool on rack 10 minutes and then remove from pan.

Serves Twelve

PER SERVING

Calories 150
Carbohydrate 23 grams
Protein 4 grams

Fat 4.5 grams (1 saturated)
Fiber 1 gram
Sodium 190 milligrams

Diabetic exchange = 1½ Carbohydrates, 1 Fat
WW point comparison = 3 points

Scientists at the Human Nutrition Center on Aging in Boston ranked blueberries as number one in antioxidant activity when compared to over forty other fruits and vegetables.

ZUCCHINI WALNUT BREAD

If you have ever grown zucchini, you know how prolific this summer squash can be. The first zucchini bread was created by someone who was looking for ways to use up zucchini. My variation on this popular bread uses pineapple to keep it wonderfully moist while allowing the spices and nuts to really stand out. Who said eating your fruits and vegetables couldn't be fun?

½ cup 1% milk	¾ cup all-purpose flour
1 large egg + 1 egg white	¾ cup Splenda Granular
4 tablespoons canola oil	1 teaspoon baking powder
1 cup grated zucchini (unpeeled)	1½ teaspoons baking soda
	1½ teaspoons cinnamon
¾ cup drained crushed pineapple	½ teaspoon nutmeg
2 teaspoons vanilla	¼ teaspoon allspice
¾ cup whole wheat flour	⅓ cup chopped walnuts

1. Preheat oven to 350°F. Coat a 9 x 5-inch loaf pan with nonstick baking spray.
2. In a medium bowl stir together the first 7 ingredients (milk through vanilla). Set aside.
3. In a large bowl combine flours, Splenda, baking powder, baking soda, spices, and nuts. Stir; make a well and add the liquid mixture, stirring just until blended. Spoon into prepared pan.
4. Bake for 40 minutes or until center springs back when lightly touched. Before removing from pan, cool on wire rack for 10 minutes.

Serves Twelve

PER SERVING

Calories 140
Carbohydrate 16 grams
Protein 4 grams

Fat 7 grams (.5 saturated)
Fiber 2 grams
Sodium 200 milligrams

Diabetic exchange = 1 Carbohydrate, 1 Fat
WW point comparison = 3 points

SOUR CREAM ALMOND POPPY SEED LOAF

I never know which recipes will tickle people's taste buds. This one certainly did for several of my tasters. Its cake-like texture melts in your mouth, and this loaf is superb when sliced and topped with fresh berries as a dessert.

¼ cup margarine, softened	Zest of one lemon
1 cup Splenda Granular	1 teaspoon almond extract
1 large egg + 2 egg whites	½ teaspoon vanilla
⅓ cup unsweetened apple-sauce	2 cups all-purpose flour
1 cup light sour cream	1 teaspoon baking powder
2 tablespoons poppy seeds	1 teaspoon baking soda

1. Preheat oven to 350°F. Coat a 9 × 5-inch loaf pan with nonstick baking spray.
2. In a large bowl cream together margarine and Splenda with an electric mixer. Beat in egg and egg whites. On slow speed blend in applesauce, sour cream, poppy seeds, zest, and almond and vanilla extracts.
3. Sift together flour, baking powder, and baking soda. Stir flour mixture into poppy seed mixture just until flour is incorporated—do not overmix. Spoon into prepared pan.
4. Bake for 45 minutes or until center springs back when lightly touched. Cool in pan on wire rack for 15 minutes before removing from pan.

Serves Twelve

PER SERVING

Calories 170
Carbohydrate 19 grams
Protein 5 grams

Fat 8 grams (2 saturated)
Fiber 1 gram
Sodium 180 milligrams

Diabetic exchange = 1½ Carbohydrate, 2 Fat
WW point comparison = 4 points

 Poppy Seed Trivia: It takes 900,000 of these seeds, which are actually kidney shaped and slate blue (if you look *real* close), to make one pound.

BUTTERMILK PECAN CRUMB CAKE

My husband is a fan of coffee cakes with traditional crumb topping. Unfortunately the amount of butter and sugar it takes to make one made him not want to indulge frequently. However, this moist crumb cake with its crunchy, sweet topping not only tastes great but is low in both fat and sugar—now he can indulge at will!

CAKE BATTER:
¾ cup buttermilk
1 large egg
2 tablespoons canola oil
⅔ cup Splenda Granular
1 teaspoon orange zest
½ teaspoon vanilla
1½ cups all-purpose flour
1½ teaspoons baking powder
½ teaspoon baking soda
½ teaspoon cinnamon
¼ teaspoon nutmeg
¼ teaspoon salt

TOPPING:
¼ cup pecans
¼ cup all-purpose flour
2 tablespoons brown sugar
2 tablespoons Splenda Granular
1 tablespoon butter, melted
½ teaspoon cinnamon

1. Preheat oven to 350°F. Coat an 8-inch round baking pan with nonstick baking spray.
2. Batter: In a medium bowl whisk together the buttermilk, egg, oil, Splenda Granular, orange zest, and vanilla. Set aside.
3. In a large bowl combine the next 6 ingredients. Stir; make a well in the center and pour in buttermilk mixture. Mix gently with a spoon until batter is smooth. Spoon batter into prepared pan.
4. Topping: In a small bowl mix together pecans, flour, brown sugar, Splenda, butter, and cinnamon. Sprinkle over top of cake.
5. Bake for 25 minutes or until toothpick inserted into center comes out clean.

Serves Eight

PER SERVING

Calories 195

Carbohydrate 28 grams

Protein 5 grams

Fat 6 grams (2 saturated)

Fiber 1 gram

Sodium 200 milligrams

Diabetic exchange = 2 Carbohydrates, 1 Fat

WW point comparison = 4 points

Traditional crumb-topped coffee cake has over 500 calories and 25 grams of fat per piece!

S'MORE CRUMB CAKE

This crumb cake makes a great afternoon snack. My kids love it. The fun combination of graham crackers and chocolate chips makes it easy to see where it got its name.

CAKE BATTER:

3 tablespoons margarine, melted

¾ cup buttermilk

1 large egg

1 teaspoon vanilla

¾ cup Splenda Granular

1½ cups all-purpose flour

1½ teaspoons baking powder

½ teaspoon baking soda

½ teaspoon cinnamon

TOPPING:

⅓ cup graham cracker crumbs

¼ cup Splenda Granular

¼ cup mini chocolate chips

2 teaspoons powdered sugar

1. Preheat oven to 350°F. Coat an 8-inch square baking pan with non-stick baking spray.
2. **CAKE BATTER:** In a medium bowl whisk together margarine, buttermilk, egg, vanilla, and Splenda. Set aside.
3. Combine flour, baking powder, baking soda, and cinnamon in a large bowl. Stir; make a well in the center and pour in buttermilk mixture. Mix gently with a spoon until batter is smooth. Spoon batter into prepared pan.
4. **TOPPING:** Combine graham cracker crumbs, Splenda, and chocolate chips. Sprinkle over cake.
5. Bake for 20 minutes or until toothpick inserted into center comes out clean.
6. Sift powdered sugar over cake.

Serves Nine

PER SERVING

Calories 180

Carbohydrate 24 grams

Protein 4 grams

Fat 7 grams (2 saturated)

Fiber 1 gram

Sodium 240 milligrams

Diabetic exchange = 1½ Carbohydrate, 1 Fat

WW point comparison = 4 points

Sensational Salads

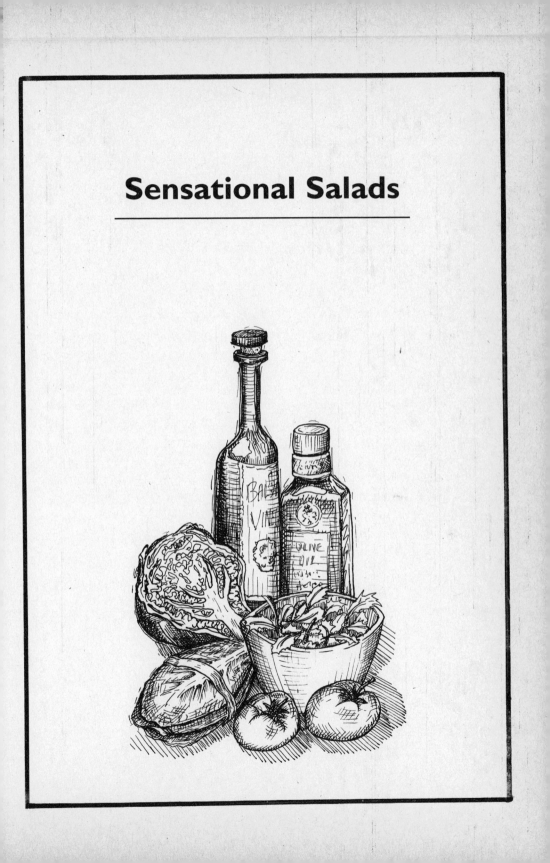

A WEIGHT-LOSS CLIENT OF MINE PROUDLY TOLD ME HE HAD SWITCHED FROM his usual lunch of sandwiches to salad-bar salads in order to lose weight. One glance at his food diary told me what I had feared: His "healthier" lunch salads had not reduced his calories at all! In fact, he may have increased his calories well above that of his usual sandwiches. Although he started out on the right track by filling his plate with lettuce and vegetables, he then piled on a variety of prepared salads, including potato salad, marinated beans, and his favorite salad—carrot and raisin. Then, he added cheese, bacon, and a dollop or two of dressing. The reality is that a trip like this to the salad bar results in a salad containing more than 1,000 calories! Loaded with mayonnaise, oil, and, often, sugar, many salad-bar favorites are heavier on fat and unwanted sugar than on healthy carbs or protein.

Fortunately, salads—when made right—can be terrific, healthy, and satisfying foods for everyone. They can fill you up—not out—adding fiber, vitamins, minerals, and a whole host of phytochemicals (healthy, disease-fighting plant-based chemicals) to your diet. And when combined with lean protein, they make a wonderful weight-loss meal. The truth is, I can hardly blame my client for his choices, because many of them are my favorites, too—so I have reinvented them. I think you will be amazed at the difference, because there is *no* difference when it comes to their great taste, but much when it comes to nutrition.

Sensational Salads and Dressings

Classic Triple Bean Salad

Creamy Carrot and Raisin Salad

Oriental Cucumber Salad

Sweet Italian Tomato Salad

Marinated Beet and Red Onion Salad

Romaine and Orange Salad

Mandarin Spinach Salad

Spinach Salad with Hot Bacon Dressing

Sweet and Sour Party Slaw

Creamy Coleslaw

Asian Peanut Slaw

Waldorf Slaw

Chinese Chicken Salad

Holiday Cranberry Gelatin Salad

Dressings

Sweet Balsamic Vinaigrette

Raspberry Vinaigrette

Thousand Island Dressing

Sesame Ginger Dressing

Fat-Free Catalina (Sweet French) Dressing

Creamy Poppy Seed Dressing

CLASSIC THREE-BEAN SALAD

My mother loves this salad-bar staple. She buys it in large jars yet is careful to watch her portions because of the sugar content. Now she can make her own using my recipe, which contains ½ the carbohydrates and calories and about ⅓ of the fat of commercially prepared versions. In her honor I have designated an ample ¾-cup portion.

1 15-ounce can cut green beans, drained	1 small red onion, diced
1 15-ounce can yellow wax beans, drained	½ cup red wine vinegar
	⅔ cup Splenda Granular
1 15-ounce kidney beans, drained and rinsed	¼ cup tomato juice
	3 tablespoons canola oil
1 small green pepper, diced	¾ teaspoon salt
1 small red pepper, diced	½ teaspoon pepper

1. In a large bowl gently mix together beans, green and red peppers, and red onion.
2. In a small bowl (or jar with lid) whisk (or shake) remaining ingredients.
3. Pour dressing over bean mixture and toss to coat. Cover and refrigerate at least 6 hours or preferably overnight before serving.

Serves Six (¾ cup)

PER SERVING

Calories 165	Fat 6.5 grams (0.5 saturated)
Carbohydrate 22 grams	Fiber 7 grams
Protein 6 gram	Sodium 360 milligrams

Diabetic exchange = 2 Vegetable, 1 Fat, 1 Very Lean Meat, ½ Carbohydrate
WW point comparison = 2 points

Not all carbs are created equal. This salad is chock-full of fiber and high in protein—in other words, these carbs are good for you.

CREAMY CARROT AND RAISIN SALAD

*My editor requested this one. She says this good old-fashioned deli favorite is
making a comeback in her area. I'm not sure it ever left.*

1/3 cup raisins	1/4 cup nonfat plain yogurt
2 cups peeled, coarsely grated carrots (or 10-ounce bag fresh shredded carrots)	3 tablespoons, Splenda Granular (or 4 Splenda packets)
1/4 cup chopped celery	2 tablespoons orange juice
1/4 cup light mayonnaise	1 tablespoon lemon juice
	1/4 teaspoon salt

1. In a small bowl pour 1/2 cup very hot water over raisins. Let sit
   5 minutes, drain, and transfer to a medium bowl. Add carrots and
   celery.
2. Whisk together remaining ingredients and toss with carrot mixture.
   Serve immediately at room temperature or refrigerate.

Serves Five (1/2 cup)

PER SERVING

Calories 90
Carbohydrate 15 grams
Protein 2 grams

Fat 3 grams (1 saturated)
Fiber 2 grams
Sodium 210 milligrams

Diabetic exchange = 1 Vegetable, 1/2 Fruit, 1 Fat
WW point comparison = 1 point

Pick this up at the deli and you will also be picking up twice the sugar and carbohydrates and four times the fat in a 1/2-cup serving.

ORIENTAL CUCUMBER SALAD

A cool and refreshing salad brimming with flavor, this is often served with Asian dishes as it offers a nice balance to their spiciness. Serve it with grilled teriyaki chicken or fish.

½ cup hot water	½ teaspoon salt
¼ cup Splenda Granular	1 small jalapeno, seeded and finely diced (optional)
¼ cup natural rice wine vinegar	1½ pounds cucumbers, peeled, seeded, and sliced (about 2½ cups)
2 tablespoons sliced green onion	
2 tablespoons minced fresh cilantro	1 medium carrot, peeled and shredded
½ teaspoon fresh grated ginger	

1. In a large shallow bowl whisk together all ingredients except cucumbers and carrot. When thoroughly mixed toss with the cucumbers and carrot.
2. Refrigerate until cool (at least 30 minutes). Serve in lettuce cups if desired.

Serves Four (½ cup)

PER SERVING

Calories 35
Carbohydrate 8 grams
Protein 1 gram

Fat 0 grams (0 saturated)
Fiber 2 grams
Sodium 260 milligrams

Diabetic exchange = 1 Vegetable
WW point comparison = 1 point

To keep cucumbers crisp, sprinkle slices with 2 teaspoons of salt and let sit for one hour. Rinse well before adding to recipe and eliminate ½ teaspoon salt added to dressing.

SWEET ITALIAN TOMATO SALAD

This is at its best when tomatoes are at the peak of their season and are firm and full of flavor. It's so good that even people who don't usually eat tomatoes enjoy it. It can be served either cold or at room temperature, making it a great buffet dish.

⅓ cup white wine (or cider) vinegar

⅓ cup Splenda Granular

3 tablespoons extra virgin olive oil

¾ teaspoon dried basil (or 2 teaspoons fresh, minced)

½ teaspoon minced garlic

¼ teaspoon salt (or to taste)

8 medium tomatoes (about 2½ pounds), quartered and seeded

1. In a large bowl whisk together all the ingredients except tomatoes. When thoroughly mixed, gently stir in tomatoes. Will keep several days covered in the refrigerator.

Serves Six (¾ cup)

PER SERVING

Calories 100
Carbohydrate 10 grams
Protein 1 gram

Fat 7 grams (1 saturated)
Fiber 2 grams
Sodium 110 milligrams

Diabetic exchange = 2 Vegetables, 1 Fat
WW point comparison = 2 points

Tomatoes are an excellent source of potassium and vitamin C. You can add buffalo mozzarella or goat cheese to this salad for extra flavor and texture.

MARINATED BEET AND RED ONION SALAD

This low-calorie salad is a refreshing and colorful change from the usual slaws and potato salads. The recipe can be doubled or tripled.

1 **16-ounce can sliced beets**	3 **tablespoons Splenda Granular (or 4 Splenda packets)**
¼ **cup beet juice (reserved from sliced beets)**	½ **teaspoon dry mustard**
½ **medium red onion, peeled and sliced thin**	½ **teaspoon cornstarch**
¼ **cup white wine (or cider) vinegar**	

1. Drain beets, reserving ¼ cup liquid, and julienne to make ½-inch strips. Place in a large bowl and add onion. Set aside.
2. In a small saucepan mix together the reserved juice and remaining ingredients. Place over medium heat and cook until sauce comes to a boil, thickens slightly, and clears. Pour marinade over beets and red onion. Cool, then refrigerate for several hours before serving.

Serves Three (½ cup)

PER SERVING

Calories 40
Carbohydrate 10 grams
Protein 1 gram

Fat 0 grams (0 saturated)
Fiber 2 grams
Sodium 170 milligrams

Diabetic exchange = 2 Vegetables
WW point comparison = 0 points

For a picnic, triple the recipe, place in a medium bowl, and garnish with 2 teaspoons fresh orange zest (will serve 10–12 as part of a buffet).

ROMAINE AND ORANGE SALAD

This light and sweet salad is the perfect complement to a heavy or spicy entrée. Don't skip toasting the nuts, as it crisps them up and brings out their flavor.

½ cup sliced almonds

2 oranges, peeled and sectioned

8 cups chopped or torn romaine lettuce

¼ cup rice wine vinegar

¼ up Splenda Granular

3 tablespoons canola oil

3 tablespoons orange juice

½ teaspoon prepared mustard
   Fresh ground pepper to taste

1. Preheat oven to 325°F. Spread almonds onto ungreased baking sheet and bake for 5 minutes. Shake sheet to toss nuts and bake 2–3 minutes longer until nuts darken in color. Set aside to cool.
2. Cut orange sections in half and place in large bowl. Add romaine and toss.
3. In a small bowl whisk together remaining ingredients. Just prior to serving, pour dressing over salad and toss lightly. Sprinkle almonds on top.

Serves Eight

PER SERVING

Calories 110
Carbohydrate 7 grams
Protein 2 grams

Fat 8 grams (0 saturated)
Fiber 2 grams
Sodium 45 milligrams

Diabetic exchange = 1 Vegetable, 2 Fat
WW point comparison = 2 points

MANDARIN SPINACH SALAD

The delicious dressing is very unique and absolutely makes the salad. To create this unusual sweet and tangy dressing, grated red onion is used. You can also turn this into an entrée for four by topping it with cooked thin-sliced top sirloin marinated in Teriyaki Sauce (page 149).

- 8 cups fresh spinach leaves (about 8 ounces)
- 1 8-ounce can sliced water chestnuts, drained
- 1 11-ounce can mandarin oranges, drained
- 8 ounces sliced mushrooms
- 1 small red onion, grated
- 3 tablespoons canola oil
- 2 tablespoons ketchup

- 2 tablespoons Splenda Granular
- 2 tablespoons apple cider vinegar
- 2 tablespoons water
- 2 teaspoons Worcestershire sauce
- 2 teaspoons soy sauce
  Fresh ground black pepper
- 1/3 cup sliced almonds or crispy rice noodles (optional)

1. In a large salad bowl gently combine spinach, water chestnuts, mandarin oranges and mushrooms. Set aside.
2. In a small bowl stir together next 8 ingredients. Gently toss dressing with salad just prior to serving. Add fresh pepper and sprinkle almonds or crispy noodles on top as desired.

Serves Eight

PER SERVING

Calories 100
Carbohydrate 12 grams
Protein 3 grams

Fat 5 grams (0 saturated)
Fiber 4 grams
Sodium 180 milligrams

Diabetic exchange = 2 vegetables, 1 Fat
WW point comparison = 2 points

Pop the onion into the refrigerator an hour or so before you grate it and you'll be less likely to tear up. The vapors, when cold, do not travel as readily. To prepare the grated onion, peel and trim the onion and then grate it with a medium-holed grater as you would a carrot.

SPINACH SALAD WITH HOT BACON DRESSING

Of all the spinach salad variations, this is my all-time favorite. I have seen some recipes that start out with as much as a half pound of bacon (for four servings—maybe that is why it is reserved for special occasions)! This healthful yet delicious version can be enjoyed all the time.

4 slices center-cut lean bacon	1 teaspoon cornstarch mixed with 2 teaspoons water
½ cup diced onion	
½ cup water	12 ounces prewashed, bagged spinach leaves (or 1 pound fresh)
⅓ cup cider vinegar	
3 tablespoons Splenda Granular (or 4 Splenda packets)	1 red onion, peeled and sliced into thin rings
Salt (to taste if desired)	1 cup sliced mushrooms

1. In a large skillet, cook bacon over moderate heat, turning until crisp. Transfer to a paper-towel-lined plate, blot off excess fat, and crumble. Set aside.
2. Add onion to drippings (there should be about 2 tablespoons—if there is more, discard excess). Cook for 3 minutes or until softened and golden. Add water, vinegar, Splenda, and salt if desired. Stir, scraping bottom to incorporate drippings.
3. Bring to low boil and add cornstarch mixture. Heat until thickened and clear.
4. In a large bowl combine spinach, onion, and mushrooms. Pour hot dressing over spinach mixture and toss. Sprinkle with crumbled bacon and serve.

Serves Eight

PER SERVING

Calories 100
Carbohydrate 12 grams
Protein 3 grams

Fat 5 grams (1 saturated)
Fiber 4 grams
Sodium 180 milligrams

Diabetic exchange = 2 vegetables, 1 Fat
WW point comparison = 2 points

Using prewashed bagged spinach makes whipping up a great spinach salad a snap.

SWEET AND SOUR PARTY SLAW

When I think of picnic food, I think slaws. Slaws are shredded vegetable salads. Most of them, though not all, include shredded cabbage as a main ingredient. Slaws are great for picnics because they are easy to make (even when serving a crowd) and, more important, easy to tote. This is one of my favorites—it uses both green and red cabbage for great color and has a sweet and tangy oil-based dressing.

6	**cups shredded* green cabbage (about 1½ pounds of cabbage)**	**3**	**tablespoons Splenda Granular (or 4 Splenda packets)**
2	**cups shredded red cabbage**	**3**	**tablespoons virgin olive oil**
1	**cup shredded carrot (use large-holed grater)**	**1**	**tablespoon creamy mustard (like Dijonnaise)**
½	**sweet onion, peeled**	**2**	**teaspoons celery seed**
¼	**cup fresh chopped parsley (or cilantro)**	**½**	**teaspoon minced garlic**
¼	**cup cider vinegar**	**½**	**teaspoon salt**
			Pepper to taste

1. Place cabbages and carrot in a large bowl. Quarter onion lengthwise. Cut into thin slices (making long thin slivers of onion). Add to bowl. Toss in parsley.
2. In a small bowl whisk together remaining ingredients. Pour over slaw and toss. Chill before serving.

Serves Eight (1 cup)

PER SERVING

Calories 70
Carbohydrate 7 grams
Protein 1 gram

Fat 5 grams (.5 saturated)
Fiber 2 grams
Sodium 180 milligrams

Diabetic exchange = 1 Vegetable, 1 Fat
WW point comparison = 1 point

*When shredding your cabbage for this beautiful salad, use a knife—not a food processor or grater. Remove outer leaves and core cabbage. Cut each half in half lengthwise (you will have four cabbage quarters). Place quarter (one of cut sides down) on a cutting board and using a long, sharp knife (like a chef's knife), slice off thin slices of cabbage—you will have beautiful long julienne shreds of cabbage. Repeat with all four pieces or until you have amount required.

CREAMY COLESLAW

If you enjoy the famous slaw found at KFC, you'll enjoy this. The big difference is not the taste but that my recipe contains one half the fat of theirs and no sugar at all.

8 cups very finely chopped cabbage	¼ cup 1% milk
1 medium carrot, peeled and shredded	¼ cup Splenda Granular
6 tablespoons light mayonnaise	2 tablespoons vinegar
6 tablespoons light sour cream	1 tablespoon lemon juice
	1 teaspoon bottled horseradish
	Generous ¼ teaspoon salt

1. Place cabbage and carrot in a large bowl. Set aside.
2. Whisk together remaining ingredients and toss with cabbage. Chill for at least 2 hours for flavors to penetrate cabbage.

Serves 8 (¾ cup)

PER SERVING

Calories 80
Carbohydrate 8 grams
Protein 1 gram

Fat 4.5 grams (0.5 saturated)
Fiber 2 grams
Sodium 210 milligrams

Diabetic exchange = 1 Vegetable, 1 Fat
WW point comparison = 1 point

This slaw is an excellent source of both vitamin A and vitamin C.

ASIAN PEANUT SLAW

Every time *I take this to a picnic or potluck I am asked for the recipe. It's definitely not your usual slaw, but it's incredibly delicious, especially to peanut butter fans. It has an Asian flare and complements fish or meat, including good ol' American favorites like hamburgers and hot dogs.*

5 cups shredded* green cabbage (about 1 pound)	**1** tablespoon brown sugar
⅓ cup green onion, sliced on diagonal	**2** teaspoons lite soy sauce
1 medium carrot, peeled and shredded	**2** teaspoons sesame oil
	1 tablespoon water
3 tablespoons natural rice vinegar	**⅛** teaspoon red pepper flakes (or to taste)
2½ tablespoons peanut butter	**2½** tablespoons chopped, unsalted peanuts for garnish
2 tablespoons Splenda Granular (or 3 Splenda packets)	Fresh cilantro (optional for garnish)

1. Place cabbage, onion, and carrot in a large bowl.
2. Vigorously whisk together remaining ingredients in a small bowl until smooth. Pour dressing over cabbage and toss. (This slaw is best served within an hour or so of tossing. Take the dressing in a separate bottle if you are "toting" it and toss at serving location.) Garnish with peanuts and cilantro.

Serves Five (1 cup)

PER SERVING

Calories 120
Carbohydrate 11 grams
Protein 4 grams

Fat 8 grams (1 saturated)
Fiber 3 grams
Sodium 120 milligrams

Diabetic exchange = 2 vegetables, 1½ Fat
WW point comparison = 2 points

* See page 110 for tip for shredding cabbage.

For a picnic, double the recipe, place in a medium bowl and garnish with cilantro. Portion sizes here are generous at 1 cup—it will serve 12–16 people as part of a buffet.

WALDORF SLAW

The original Waldorf salad was created at New York's Waldorf-Astoria Hotel, in the late 1890s. It contained simply apples, celery, and mayonnaise. Inspired by the original recipe, I have created a Waldorf slaw significantly lower in carbs and fat. I especially like the great crunch and beautiful color added by the red cabbage.

2 cups shredded red cabbage	6 tablespoons low-fat plain yogurt
1 cup diced peeled apples	
1 cup diced celery	1 tablespoon Splenda Granular (or 2 Splenda packet)
⅓ up chopped walnuts	
5 tablespoons light mayonnaise	¼ teaspoon salt

1. Place cabbage, apples, celery, and nuts in a large bowl.
2. Whisk together remaining ingredients and toss with cabbage mixture. Refrigerate to chill and serve.

Serves Six (¾ cup)

PER SERVING

Calories 100
Carbohydrate 8 grams
Protein 2 grams

Fat 8 grams (1 saturated)
Fiber 2 grams
Sodium 190 milligrams

Diabetic exchange = 1 Vegetable, 1½ Fat
WW point comparison = 2 points

CHINESE CHICKEN SALAD

I simply had to include this recipe because I love Chinese Chicken Salad. While such a salad sounds light, most are anything but. In fact, a popular fast-food chain's oriental-inspired chicken salad with sesame dressing contains over 35 grams of fat and uses no less than 4 different types of sugar to sweeten the dressing—for over 50 grams of carbohydrate per serving. This flavorful, large meal-sized salad packs in more protein and great nutrition with a lot less carb and calories.

4 cups spring salad mix	3 tablespoons natural rice wine vinegar
1 cup shredded Napa cabbage	1½ tablespoons Splenda Granular (or 2 Splenda packets)
1 medium red pepper, julienned	
1 medium yellow pepper, julienned	1 tablespoon lite soy sauce
2 ounces fresh snow peas, trimmed and cut in half on diagonal	½ teaspoon fresh grated ginger
	2 tablespoons canola oil
½ cup sliced green onions	1½ tablespoons sesame oil
4 cups thin strips or shredded cooked chicken breast (about 1 pound)	Fresh ground pepper
	½ cup crispy rice noodles (or sliced almonds*)

1. In a large bowl toss together the salad mix, cabbage, peppers, snow peas, and green onions. Add chicken to bowl. Set aside.
2. Whisk together remaining ingredients except rice noodles and pour into bowl. Toss lightly and portion onto 4 plates. Top each salad with 2 tablespoons noodles (or nuts).

Serves Four

PER SERVING

Calories 320
Carbohydrate 13 grams
Protein 33 grams

Fat 15 grams (2 saturated)
Fiber 3 grams
Sodium 390 milligrams

Diabetic exchange = 4 Lean Meat, 1 Vegetable, ½ Carbohydrate, 1 Fat
WW point comparison = 7 points (a packet of fast-food dressing alone is 8 points!)

*If you are severely restricting your carbs, choose almonds instead of noodles and the carbohydrates decrease to 10 grams and the fiber increases to 5 grams, making the net carbs = 5. This, however, will also increase the calories by 40 and the fat by 5 grams.

HOLIDAY CRANBERRY GELATIN SALAD

Gelatin salads like this one are like having a touch of dessert with your dinner, which is probably why they are served at festive occasions. This particular type of gelatin salad is a holiday staple, but my version also leaves you room for dessert!

1 **12-ounce bag fresh cranberries, washed and picked over**	1/4 **cup granulated sugar**
	1 **cup cold water**
1 1/2 **cups Splenda Granular**	1 1/2 **cups crushed pineapple (packed in light juice), drained**
2 **cups boiling water**	
1 **6-ounce box sugar-free cherry gelatin dessert mix**	1/2 **cup finely chopped celery**
	1/2 **cup chopped nuts**

1. Finely chop cranberries in food processor or by hand and place in medium bowl. Add Splenda and stir. Set aside.
2. In a large bowl pour boiling water over gelatin and sugar to dissolve. Add cold water. Stir in cranberries, pineapple, celery, and nuts. Pour into 2-quart serving container, mold, or 9 × 13-inch pan and place in refrigerator for several hours or until firm.

Serves Ten (1/2 cup)

PER SERVING

Calories 110
Carbohydrate 17 grams
Protein 3 grams

Fat 3.5 grams (2 saturated)
Fiber 2 grams
Sodium 45 milligrams

Diabetic exchange = 1 Carbohydrate, 1/2 Fat
WW point comparison = 2 points

If you are eating the traditional version and are watching your carbs, beware— it packs 63 grams a serving. (That's as much as eating a big piece of fruit pie!)

SWEET BALSAMIC VINAIGRETTE

This sweet vinaigrette is a lovely dressing for salads containing fruit. I like it drizzled over baby greens and sliced strawberries, spinach with fresh orange sections, or red leaf lettuce and thin pear slices.

3 tablespoons red wine vinegar	1 clove garlic, minced
2 tablespoons balsamic vinegar	3 tablespoons extra virgin
2 tablespoons orange juice	olive oil
2 tablespoons Splenda	2 teaspoons Dijon mustard
Granular (or 3 Splenda	Fresh ground pepper
packets)	

1. Whisk first 5 ingredients together in a small bowl. Whisk in olive oil one tablespoon at a time to thoroughly incorporate. Whisk in mustard. Add pepper to taste.

Serves Six (about 2 tablespoons)

PER SERVING

Calories 70
Carbohydrate 2 grams
Protein 0 grams

Fat 7 grams (1 saturated)
Fiber 0 grams
Sodium 0 milligrams

Diabetic exchange = 1½ Fat
WW point comparison = 2 points

Traditional vinaigrette recipes use three parts oil to one part vinegar, giving them up to 20 grams of fat in 2 tablespoons.

RASPBERRY VINAIGRETTE

Many raspberry vinaigrettes start with raspberry vinegar. After searching for it in my local markets, I realized that it can be both hard to find and expensive. My solution is to use whole raspberries to impart the distinctive raspberry taste. An added bonus is the thickness you get from pureeing the whole raspberries in this flavorful, reduced-fat dressing.

4 tablespoons natural rice vinegar	1 tablespoon each lime (or lemon) juice and water
2 tablespoons canola oil	1 tablespoon Splenda Granular (or 2 Splenda packets)
¼ cup fresh or frozen raspberries	
1 tablespoon Dijon mustard	Fresh ground pepper to taste

1. Puree all ingredients in a food processor or blender until smooth. Adjust pepper.

Serves Five (2 tablespoons)

PER SERVING

Calories 60
Carbohydrate 1 gram
Protein 0 grams

Fat 6 grams (0 saturated)
Fiber 1 gram
Sodium 40 milligrams

Diabetic exchange = 1 Fat
WW point comparison = 1 point

This is delicious over grilled chicken on mixed greens, garnished with toasted pecans.

THOUSAND ISLAND DRESSING

One of my all-time favorite salads is the Crab Louie. The truth is, it is the Thousand Island dressing customarily served with it that I adore. I am happy to report that this healthy version has a taste that is just as good.

½ cup light mayonnaise (I prefer Best Foods or Hellmann's)

2 tablespoons chili sauce

1 tablespoon Splenda Granular (or 1 Splenda packet)

2 tablespoons finely chopped celery

1–2 teaspoons 1% milk

1. Whisk all ingredients together in a small bowl. Thin if desired with milk.

Serves Five (2 tablespoons)

PER SERVING

Calories 45
Carbohydrate 4 grams
Protein 0 grams

Fat 3.5 grams (0 saturated)
Fiber 1 gram
Sodium 180 milligrams

Diabetic exchange = 1 Fat
WW point comparison = 1 point

SESAME GINGER DRESSING

Oil creates the emulsion in most dressings. When you cut back on the oil, the result is a thinner dressing. This cooked oriental-inspired dressing uses cornstarch as a thickener instead of a lot of oil.

⅓ cup chicken broth	1½ teaspoons fresh ginger, minced
¼ cup pineapple juice	
3 tablespoons natural rice vinegar	½ teaspoon garlic, minced
2 tablespoons sesame oil	1 teaspoon cornstarch mixed with 1 tablespoon water
1 tablespoon lite soy sauce	
2 tablespoons Splenda Granular (or 3 Splenda packets)	

1. Place all ingredients except cornstarch mixture in a small saucepan and bring to medium heat. Stir in cornstarch mixture, bring to boil, and cook until dressing is thick and clear. Remove from heat and cool. Cover and refrigerate. Shake or stir before using.

Serves Six (2 tablespoons)

PER SERVING

Calories 55
Carbohydrate 3 grams
Protein 0 grams

Fat 4.5 grams (0 saturated)
Fiber 1 gram
Sodium 140 milligrams

Diabetic exchange = 1 Fat
WW point comparison = 1 point

FAT-FREE CATALINA (SWEET FRENCH) DRESSING

Traditionally, this dressing is a sweet and tangy blend of oil, ketchup, and sugar, so it's basically fat and sugar—no wonder it's so popular! Luckily, it can be made without fat or sugar and still taste great. You must taste it to believe it.

1 cup cold water	½ teaspoon salt
1/3 cup Splenda Granular	⅛ teaspoon garlic powder
3 tablespoons tomato paste	⅛ teaspoon chili powder
1½ teaspoons cornstarch	(optional)

1. Place all the ingredients in a small saucepan and whisk until the cornstarch is completely dissolved. Place over low heat and cook until dressing comes to a boil and thickens and clears. Remove from heat and cool. Cover and refrigerate.

Serves Eight (2 tablespoons)

PER SERVING

Calories 10
Carbohydrate 3 grams
Protein 0 grams

Fat 0 grams (0 saturated)
Fiber 0 grams
Sodium 180 milligrams

Diabetic exchange = 1 Fat
WW point comparison = 1 point

Two tablespoons of bottled Honey French dressing will set you back 170 calories, 13 grams of fat, and 12 grams of carbohydrate.

CREAMY POPPY SEED DRESSING

If you like a very creamy dressing, this one is for you. It is perfect to drizzle over delicate lettuces, such as butter or Bibb, or to toss with fresh fruit.

½ cup buttermilk

½ cup light sour cream

3 tablespoons Splenda Granular (or 4 Splenda packets

2 teaspoons lemon juice

1 teaspoon poppy seeds

1. In a small bowl whisk together all ingredients.

Serves Eight (2 tablespoons)

PER SERVING

Calories 10
Carbohydrate 3 grams
Protein 0 grams

Fat 0 grams (0 saturated)
Fiber 0 grams
Sodium 180 milligrams

Diabetic exchange = 1 Fat
WW point comparison = 1 point

 Add a touch of orange zest to the dressing and serve it over fresh strawberries for a sweet finish to your meal.

Versatile Vegetables

RECENT RESEARCH SHOWS THAT, IN ADDITION TO VITAMINS, MINERALS, AND fiber, vegetables are loaded with phytochemicals (healthful plant chemicals), which are proven to help fight off everything from heart disease to cancer. Vegetables are also great when it comes to watching your waistline, as they are low in both fat and calories—until we start to dress them up for special occasions and holiday meals. It just wouldn't seem like Thanksgiving without yams or sweet potatoes, and a picnic's not a picnic without baked beans. The problem is that these traditional favorites have truly been "dressed" for the occasion. Adorned with sugar and fat, they are a far cry from Mother Nature's bounty. For example, the holiday classic sweet potato puff or soufflé—mashed sweet potatoes whipped with sugar, butter, lots of whole eggs and spices, topped with *more* sugar, more butter, and nuts. The cost of this classic: 440 calories, over 20 grams of fat, and 60 grams of carbohydrate (40 of them from sugar)—in just one serving! On page 133, you will find a mouthwatering alternative—Butternut Squash Soufflé. I guarantee you will be proud to serve it. Naturally sweet (and less carbohydrate rich) butternut squash is whipped with Splenda, a touch of butter, creamy light sour cream, one egg, three egg whites, spices, and is topped with more Splenda, a touch more butter, and just enough nuts for that fabulous finish. The cost for *this* incredible side dish: 130 calories, 6 grams of fat, and 15 grams of carbohydrate (3 of them from natural sugars). Now that's a savings that's hard to ignore.

In this chapter you will find many of your old favorites, like Boston Baked Beans (page 135), and hopefully some new ones, like the Asian Pepper Medley (page 128). Versatile enough to be served with lots of different entrees, I am sure you will find many occasions to enjoy them. Now you have no excuse not to eat your vegetables.

ERSATILE VEGETABLES

Silly Carrots

Glazed Carrots with Fresh Dill

Asian Pepper Medley

Sesame Green Beans

Orange-Sauced Beets

Sweet and Sour Red Cabbage

Sweet Potatoes with Apple Cider Syrup

Butternut Squash Soufflé

Boston Baked Beans

Stovetop Maple Sugar Baked Beans

German Potato, Green Bean, and Mushroom Salad

Sweet Southwestern-Style Corn Pudding

Buttermilk Cornbread

SILLY CARROTS

When I told my mom I was including recipes for vegetables in this book, she immediately told me about a recipe for carrots that could use a "sugar makeover." She recounted how this recipe was a huge hit at potlucks quite a few years back. I found that Silly Carrots were actually a "My Best Recipe" winner in 1981, in the Los Angeles Times *newspaper. The original recipe has a terrific sweet sauce that really makes them special. Now here is my version, which also has the same great taste. Why they are called Silly I still don't know.*

6 cups carrots, peeled and sliced (2 pounds raw carrots)	1½ teaspoons prepared mustard
1 10-ounce can tomato soup (Campbell's Healthy Selections)	1 medium onion, diced
	1 medium green pepper, diced
⅔ cup Splenda Granular	½ cup celery, chopped
⅔ cup vinegar	⅛ teaspoon salt
2 tablespoons canola oil	

1. In a medium saucepan cook carrots in boiling water just until tender (about 10 minutes). Drain and set aside.
2. Combine remaining ingredients in saucepan and cook over medium heat until boiling. Reduce heat and simmer for 10 minutes. Pour over drained carrots. Can be served hot or refrigerated and served cold.

Serves Ten (generous ½ cup)

PER SERVING

Calories 90
Carbohydrate 15 grams
Protein 2 grams

Fat 3.5 grams (0 saturated)
Fiber 3 grams
Sodium 180 milligrams

Diabetic exchange = 2½ Vegetable, 1 Fat
WW point comparison = 1 point

A single serving of Silly Carrots provides a whopping 420 percent of the Recommended Daily Allowance for vitamin A.

GLAZED CARROTS WITH FRESH DILL

Glazed carrots seem to pair well with almost any dish—maybe that is why they are so popular. Although carrots sometimes get a bad rap for their "high sugar content," they are actually low in carbohydrate and fit easily into most diets. The problem with glazed carrots is not the carrots, but the glaze. There are recipes that call for up to 1/2 cup of sugar and 1/2 cup of butter (for six servings or less!). This recipe uses just enough sweetener and butter to enhance the natural goodness of the carrots. The crowning touch is definitely the fresh dill.

1/4 cup orange juice

1/4 cup water

1 pound carrots (about 6 large), trimmed, peeled, and sliced

2 tablespoons light butter, melted

3 tablespoons Splenda Granular

1 teaspoon fresh minced dill

Salt and pepper to taste

1. Place orange juice and water in a medium saucepan. Add carrots and simmer, covered, for 15 minutes until carrots are tender and liquid is absorbed.
2. In a small bowl combine melted butter, Splenda, and dill. Pour over hot carrots and toss. Adjust salt and pepper to taste.

Serves Six (1/2 cup)

PER SERVING

Calories 60
Carbohydrate 9 grams
Protein 1 gram

Fat 2 grams (1 saturated)
Fiber 2 grams
Sodium 45 milligrams

Diabetic exchange = 1 1/2 Vegetables, 1/2 Fat
WW point comparison = 1 point

Carrots are good for you—1/2 cup of boiled carrots has only 8 grams of carbohydrate (with 2 grams of fiber) and an entire day's worth of vitamin A!

ASIAN PEPPER MEDLEY

This medley of colorful sweet peppers makes a terrific accompaniment to any grilled meat or fish. The sesame oil in this dish really adds an exotic flavor.

2   teaspoons canola oil

1   teaspoon minced garlic

3   large bell peppers, preferably 1 red, 1 green, and 1 orange or yellow, seeded and sliced into ¼-inch strips

3   tablespoons natural rice wine vinegar

1   tablespoon light soy sauce

1   tablespoon sesame oil

1   tablespoon Splenda Granular

¼   teaspoon minced or grated ginger

Fresh ground pepper

1. In a large nonstick sauté pan heat oil; add garlic and then pepper strips. Sauté over high heat for 3 minutes.
2. Mix remaining ingredients together and pour over peppers. Cook for 3–5 more minutes until peppers are tender but not limp. Season with pepper to taste.

Serves Four (generous ½ cup)

PER SERVING

Calories 70
Carbohydrate 8 grams
Protein 1 gram

Fat 4.5 grams (0 saturated)
Fiber 2 grams
Sodium 130 milligrams

Diabetic exchange = 1 Vegetable, 1 Fat
WW point comparison = 1 point

SESAME GREEN BEANS

Parboiling green beans brightens their color and keeps them plump. It also allows you to prepare the beans in advance, leaving only a last minute sauté prior to serving. I like to serve these dark and fragrant beans with Asian Barbecued Pork (page 173).

1 pound fresh green beans, trimmed	2 tablespoons Splenda Granular
1 tablespoon sesame seeds	1 tablespoon natural rice wine vinegar
2 teaspoons sesame oil	
2 tablespoons light soy sauce	Pinch of red pepper flakes

1. Place beans in a large pot of boiling water and 2 teaspoons salt for 4 minutes or until tender but still slightly firm. Drain and place in ice water until beans are cool. Drain and pat dry. Set aside.
2. In a large non-stick sauté pan toast sesame seeds until golden over low heat. Remove from pan and set aside. Add oil to pan and heat until very hot (but not smoking). Add beans and sauté for 1–2 minutes or until hot.
3. Mix together remaining ingredients and add to pan. Sauté until beans are coated and sauce is hot. Pour onto serving platter and top with toasted sesame seeds.

Serves Four

PER SERVING

Calories 70	Fat 3.5 grams (0 saturated)
Carbohydrate 9 grams	Fiber 3 grams
Protein 2 grams	Sodium 250 milligrams

Diabetic exchange = 1½ Vegetable, 1 Fat
WW point comparison = 1 point

While sesame oil is remarkably stable, sesame seeds can turn rancid due to their high oil content. Kept in a cool, dark place, they keep fresh for 3 months, in the refrigerator for 6 months, and in the freezer for up to 12 months.

ORANGE-SAUCED BEETS

I must confess, before developing this recipe I had never cooked fresh beets. What a mistake! While canned beets work just fine for this recipe, I highly recommend fresh, as their texture and flavor can't be beet (I mean beat). This richly colored side dish is versatile enough to complement the most simple to the most elegant of meals.

1	pound fresh beets or 2 15-ounce cans whole beets in juice, drained	1	teaspoon cornstarch
¼	cup orange juice	1	teaspoon orange zest
¼	cup Splenda Granular		Dash of salt
2	tablespoons white or cider vinegar	1	tablespoon margarine or butter

1. To prepare fresh beets, scrub and trim the stem down to 1 inch (tail can be left intact). Place in boiling water and boil for 40–60 minutes or until tender when pierced all the way through with a sharp knife. Drain and plunge them into cold water until cooled. Rub beets between your hands to remove peels and chop into large bite-sized cubes.
2. In a medium saucepan whisk together remaining ingredients, except margarine. Heat over medium heat until sauce comes to a boil and thickens. Turn down heat and swirl in margarine. Add beets to sauce and heat until coated and hot.

Serves Four

PER SERVING

Calories 85
Carbohydrate 14 grams
Protein 2 grams

Fat 2.5 grams (.5 saturated)
Fiber 2 grams
Sodium 150 milligrams

Diabetic exchange = 2 vegetables, ½ Fat
WW point comparison = 1 point

You may want to wear gloves to peel the beets, as the pigment will temporarily stain your hands (and anything else it touches).

SWEET AND SOUR RED CABBAGE

I remember, when I was a child, how delighted my German father was every time my mother served red cabbage. Now, when the weather turns cool in the fall, I serve this beautiful sugar-free rendition with pork loin—and my husband is delighted.

2 teaspoons olive or canola oil	½ cup red wine
½ cup diced red onion	¼ cup cider vinegar
1 medium red cabbage (about 2 pounds), cored, quartered, and thinly sliced	1 cup water
	¼ cup Splenda Granular
	½ teaspoon salt
1 apple, peeled and grated (optional)*	3-4 drops liquid smoke
	Pepper to taste

1. Heat oil in a medium-sized saucepan. Add onion and sauté 4–5 minutes or until translucent. Add cabbage, apple, wine, vinegar, water, and Splenda. Cover and simmer for 20 minutes, stirring occasionally. Stir in salt and liquid smoke and cook for 10 more minutes or until tender but still firm.

Serves Six (¾–1 cup)

PER SERVING

Calories 80
Carbohydrate 10 grams
Protein 2 grams

Fat 2 grams (.5 saturated)
Fiber 2 grams
Sodium 220 milligrams

Diabetic exchange = 2 Vegetables, ½ Fat
WW point comparison = 1 point

*Apple adds a delicious taste, 10 calories, and 3 grams of carbohydrate to each serving.

Liquid Smoke is a seasoning made through a natural process from hickory smoke concentrate. It has no calories and imparts a smoky taste, reminiscent of bacon, to foods. Be sure to use it sparingly, as it is quite concentrated.

SWEET POTATOES WITH APPLE CIDER SYRUP

If you have had enough of over-the-top-sweet marshmallow-and-brown sugar sweet potato recipes, try this one. I took the classic pairing of apples and sweet potatoes and added apple cider to create a delicious butter syrup that complements the sweet potatoes instead of overpowering them.

4 large sweet potatoes or yams (about 1½ pounds)	½ cup Splenda Granular
¾ cup apple cider	2 tablespoons butter

1. Preheat oven to 350°F.
2. Boil sweet potatoes for 20–25 minutes or until nearly tender when pierced with a knife. Drain potatoes and let stand until cool enough to handle. Peel and cut potatoes into ¼-inch rounds and layer in rectangular baking dish.
3. In a small saucepan heat apple cider over medium heat until mixture reduces by ⅓ to ½. Stir in Splenda and heat 1 more minute. Remove from heat and stir in butter. Pour syrup over potatoes, cover, and bake 30 minutes until very soft and hot.

Serves Six (½ cup)

PER SERVING

Calories 150	Fat 4.5 grams (3 saturated)
Carbohydrate 27 grams	Fiber 2 grams
Protein 2 grams	Sodium 50 milligrams

Diabetic exchange = 2 Vegetables, ½ Fat
WW point comparison = 3 points

Although sweet potatoes may taste like they contain more sugar than their white cousins, they actually affect blood sugar much more slowly. Top them with ½ cup or more of brown sugar and a slew of marshmallows and that all changes. In fact, one serving of the traditional sweet potato casserole has over 60 grams of carbohydrate (over 30 of them from sugar).

BUTTERNUT SQUASH SOUFFLÉ

If you want a lower-carb alternative to sweet potatoes, look no further. This simple-to-make yet sumptuous side dish tastes creamy, rich, and sweet and yet has a fraction of the sugar, fat, and calories of traditional versions. Don't worry, I have even included the nut-studded crunchy topping. I guarantee you, no one will think this is low in anything.

SOUFFLÉ

3 cups cooked mashed butternut squash (about 2 pounds whole)

⅔ cup Splenda Granular

1 large egg

3 egg whites

⅓ cup light sour cream

1 tablespoon margarine, melted

¾ teaspoon cinnamon

½ teaspoon vanilla

1 teaspoon baking powder

¼ teaspoon salt

TOPPING

2 tablespoons flour

3 tablespoons Splenda Granular

3 tablespoons pecans, finely chopped

1 tablespoon margarine, melted

¼ teaspoon cinnamon

1. Preheat oven to 350.°F Coat a 2-quart casserole or soufflé dish with nonstick cooking spray.
2. Prepare squash; prick squash with a knife in several places and place in microwave (whole). Microwave on high for 8–10 minutes. Remove and cut squash in half lengthwise. When cool enough to handle, scoop out seeds. Place halves, cut-side down, in a glass baking dish, add ¼ cup of water, cover tightly with plastic wrap (or lid), and place back in microwave for 10 more minutes or until flesh is very soft. Scoop out flesh into large bowl.
3. Add remaining soufflé ingredients and beat until well blended. Spoon into baking dish and smooth top.
4. In a small bowl combine all topping ingredients and mix with fork or fingers until crumbly. Cover top of soufflé with crumb mixture.
5. Bake for 30–35 minutes until soufflé puffs up in center and top is well browned.

Serves Eight (½ cup)

PER SERVING

Calories 120

Carbohydrate 15 grams

Protein 4 grams

Fat 5 grams (2 saturated)

Fiber 3 grams

Sodium 180 milligrams

Diabetic exchange = 1 Carbohydrate, 1 Fat

WW point comparison = 2 points

One half cup of mashed butternut squash contains 13 grams of carbohydrate. Compare that to ½ cup mashed sweet potatoes at 40 grams of carbohydrate.

BOSTON BAKED BEANS

Yes, Boston Baked beans are named after the city of Boston, where the early American settlers had an affinity for slow cooking beans with molasses and lard or pork fat. Today, baked beans have become the quintessential side dish to hamburgers and hot dogs across the country.

1 **pound dried navy beans, rinsed and picked clean of stones or debris**	3 **tablespoons molasses**
	2 **tablespoons cider vinegar**
	2 **teaspoons dry mustard**
1 **large onion, chopped**	¾ **teaspoon salt**
½ **cup tomato juice**	½ **teaspoon ginger**
½ **cup sugar-free maple syrup**	**liquid smoke (optional)**
⅔ **cup Splenda Granular**	

1. Bring 2 quarts of water and beans to boil in a large pot and simmer 2 minutes. Remove from heat, cover, and soak for at least 1 hour (up to eight hours).
2. Preheat oven to 300°F. Drain beans and add them to a pot, casserole, or bean pot. Add remaining ingredients. Stir and thoroughly cover beans with hot water (about 2 cups).
3. Cover and bake 5–6 hours or until beans are tender and sauce bubbly, checking midpoint to see if more water is needed.

Serves Twelve (½ cup)

PER SERVING

Calories 140
Carbohydrate 26 grams
Protein 8 grams

Fat 0 grams (2 saturated)
Fiber 7 grams
Sodium 180 milligrams

Diabetic exchange = 1½ Carbohydrates
WW point comparison = 1 point

Fiber blunts the rapid rise in blood sugar associated with refined carbohydrates. Beans are an incredible source of fiber (and a nice protein source as well), making them very good carbs.

STOVETOP MAPLE SUGAR BAKED BEANS

In today's fast-paced world, "quick" and "easy" are very welcome words indeed. In the time it takes to make the rest of your meal you can have "home-made" baked beans. These beans are truly quick and easy.

1 teaspoon canola oil	1 teaspoon vinegar
1 small onion, finely chopped	4–5 drops liquid smoke
1/2 cup tomato sauce	2 15-ounce cans pinto beans, drained and rinsed (you can vary the beans if you choose)
1/4 cup sugar-free maple syrup	
1/4 cup Splenda Granular	
1 tablespoons molasses	
2 teaspoons prepared mustard	

1. In a large saucepan heat oil, add onions, and sauté for 3–4 minutes until softened slightly. Add remaining ingredients and stir. Simmer on low for 25–30 minutes.

Serves Six

PER SERVING

Calories 145
Carbohydrate 26 grams
Protein 8 grams

Fat 2 grams (2 saturated)
Fiber 5 grams
Sodium 160 milligrams

Diabetic exchange = 1 1/2 Carbohydrates
WW point comparison = 1 point

GERMAN POTATO, GREEN BEAN, AND MUSHROOM SALAD

 *German potato salad, dense in starchy white potatoes and bacon, isn't on anyone's healthy food list, especially if you're watching your carbohydrate and fat intake. But boy can it taste good! I have made several adjustments to this favorite to put it back on the menu. I lightened the density by adding lower-carbohydrate vegetables, then lessened the amount of bacon (being sure to leave enough for that classic taste) and took out the sugar. Enjoy it anytime. Try pairing it with reduced-fat sausage or brats for a German feast.*

8 ounces fresh green beans, trimmed	⅓ cup white wine vinegar or cider vinegar
1 pound red potatoes, scrubbed	2 tablespoons Splenda Granular
3 slices center-cut bacon	⅛ teaspoon salt (or more to taste)
1 small onion, diced	4 ounces fresh mushrooms cut into wide ¼-inch slices
½ teaspoon dry mustard	Black pepper to taste
½ teaspoon crushed thyme	
2 teaspoons flour	
⅔ cup chicken broth	

1. Boil green beans in a large pot of water with 1 teaspoon salt for 6–8 minutes until tender but still crisp. Remove with slotted spoon into a large covered bowl and add potatoes (with skins) to water. Boil for 20 minutes or until potatoes are tender when pierced with a fork. Drain, slice, and place in covered bowl with green beans. While potatoes are boiling, cook bacon until crisp in a large skillet. Remove bacon, drain off fat with paper towels, crumble, and set aside.

2. Pour all but 2 tablespoons of drippings out of pan. Add onion and sauté until soft. Stir in mustard and thyme and then flour. Whisk in broth, vinegar, Splenda, and salt. Stir until thickened. Add mushrooms, briefly, to heat, *not* cook, and pour hot sauce over potato mixture. Toss, add crumbled bacon, and adjust seasonings.

Serves Six

PER SERVING

Calories 130   Fat 3.5 grams (.5 saturated)
Carbohydrate 20 grams   Fiber 3 grams
Protein 5 grams   Sodium 290 milligrams

Diabetic exchange = 1 Carbohydrate, 1 Vegetable, ½ Fat
WW point comparison = 2 points

SWEET SOUTHWESTERN-STYLE CORN PUDDING

Corn pudding recipes vary quite a bit yet all are high in calories, fat, and carbohydrates. Some are made with great quantities of milk and eggs and are more like a custard, while others are so heavy with cornmeal that they can be cut into squares. One of the most popular recipes uses a commercial cornbread mix, canned corn, butter, and milk or sour cream. It has a nice "middle of the road" texture and both a sweet and rich flavor. It is this version I have re-created with the addition of sautéed onion and green chilies. The result is a fantastic side dish that is perfect with Mexican food or grilled food flavored with Southwest spices. If you prefer a more classic version simply use the traditional version below.

1	small onion, diced	1	15-ounce can corn, drained
2	tablespoons margarine or butter	½	cup cornmeal
1	cup buttermilk	2	tablespoons all-purpose flour
1	large egg + 2 egg whites	½	teaspoon baking powder
1	4.5-ounce can chopped green chilies	½	cup Splenda Granular

1. Preheat oven to 350°F. Spray a 1-quart casserole dish with nonstick cooking spray.
2. In a small sauté pan cook onion in margarine until soft. Scrape onions into large bowl and add buttermilk, egg, egg whites, and chilies. Place corn into food processor or blender. Pulse or blenderize briefly to coarsely chop corn. Add corn to bowl.
3. In a small bowl blend remaining dry ingredients. Pour into liquid mixture and stir. Spoon batter into prepared dish and bake for 45–50 minutes or until puffed and browned.

TRADITIONAL VERSION: Eliminate the onions and chilies. Melt margarine or butter and add to liquid mixture. (No significant change in calories, fat, or carbohydrate.)

Serves Six

PER SERVING

Calories 140
Carbohydrate 18 grams
Protein 5 grams

Fat 4 grams (2 saturated)
Fiber 2 grams
Sodium 270 milligrams

Diabetic exchange = 1 Carbohydrate, 1 Fat
WW point comparison = 2 points

BUTTERMILK CORNBREAD

Entire books have been written to pay homage to this seemingly simple side dish. More than just a bread to many, cornbread is comfort. And like most comfort foods, there are lots of styles that will satisfy. I have fashioned mine after that of a famous pie shop that became even more famous for its cornbread (Marie Callander's for those of you guessing). Loved by y'all, it's moist, sweet, and not too heavy. Serve it up warm for a real treat.

1 large egg + 2 egg whites	1 cup all-purpose flour
3 tablespoons margarine, melted	½ cup Splenda Granular
	4 teaspoons baking powder
1¼ cups buttermilk	½ teaspoon baking soda
1 teaspoon vanilla	Pinch of salt
1 cup cornmeal	

1. Preheat oven to 375°F. Spray an 8-inch square pan or 9-inch round pan with nonstick cooking spray.
2. In a medium bowl whisk together first 4 ingredients (eggs through vanilla). Set aside.
3. In a large bowl combine the dry ingredients. Stir; make a well in the center and pour in buttermilk mixture. Mix gently with a spoon just until all dry ingredients are wet. Spoon batter into prepared pan. Bake for 20–25 minutes or until center springs back when lightly touched.

Serves Twelve

PER SERVING

Calories 125	Fat 3.5 grams (2 saturated)
Carbohydrate 19 grams	Fiber 1 gram
Protein 4 grams	Sodium 295 milligrams

Diabetic exchange = 1 Carbohydrate, 1 Fat
WW point comparison = 2 points

This ubiquitous vegetable can be found in over 3,000 grocery-store products! A single ear of corn averages 800 kernels, which fit neatly into 16 rows.

Great Condiments

CONDIMENTS MAKE ORDINARY FOOD EXTRAORDINARY BY COMPLEMENT-ING and adding flavor to food. Whether sweet, spicy, savory, chunky, or creamy, it is often the sauce, dressing, or topping that makes a dish memorable. Unfortunately, many condiments add more than flavor—they also can add unwanted fat, sugar, or calories—the "hidden" calories or carbs that you barely notice (until you step on the scale). That being said, it doesn't mean I think healthy food should be served plain. My belief is that when you reduce the fat in food you need to *boost* the flavor to give your palate something to grab on to and excite it. This flavor element is the key to preparing delicious but healthy foods. I had a fun time creating this chapter because it gave me the chance to add a variety of great flavors to jazz up everything from entreés to desserts.

You will find the sugar and fat savings in these recipes are enormous when you compare them to traditional condiments. For example, a single side serving of the holiday staple cranberry sauce can have as much as 45 grams of carbohydrate. (If you have diabetes, that is equal to 3 servings of fruit or more than half of your total meal's carbohydrate allowance.) The Two-Way Cranberry Sauce (page 151) will set you back only half of a fruit or 8 grams of carbohydrates. A serving of 2 tablespoons of Quick Smooth Barbecue Sauce (page 145) becomes a "free" food with a mere 15 calories and 4 grams of carbs, as does pungent and creamy Sweet Horseradish Sauce with only 1 gram of fat and 1 gram of carbohydrate. I love the great full flavors I was able to create as well as the versatility of so many of these recipes. Some personal favorites are the Thai Peanut Sauce, Tomato Ginger Jam, and the Bread and Butter Pickles. I am sure you will soon find many favorites to claim as your own—with my complements.

GREAT CONDIMENTS

Sweet Smoky Barbecue Sauce

Quick Smooth Barbecue Sauce

Thai Peanut Sauce

Sweet Horseradish Sauce

Sweet Mustard Sauce and Dip

Teriyaki Sauce

Spicy Teriyaki Sauce

Two Way Cranberry Sauce

Sensational No-Cook Cranberry Relish

Cranberry Chutney

Peach Chutney

Tomato Ginger Jam

Low-Sugar Strawberry Freezer Jam

Microwave Cinnamon Applesauce

Bread and Butter Pickles

SWEET SMOKY BARBECUE SAUCE

Traditional American barbecue sauce is not only versatile but also extremely popular. But no matter what the style—hickory, smoky, honey, or spicy—there is one ingredient all these sauces have in common: sugar. And while a tablespoon may fit into your diet, many of us eat far more than a tablespoon (or two) at a sitting. This simple-to-make sauce is a great low-sugar complement to beef, pork or chicken.

2 teaspoons oil	⅓ cup Splenda Granular
1 teaspoon minced garlic	2 teaspoons molasses
1 cup finely chopped onion	1 teaspoon chili powder
1 6-ounce can tomato paste	1 teaspoon dry mustard
1 cup water	3-4 drops liquid smoke
2 tablespoons apple cider vinegar	Few drops of Tabasco sauce (optional, to taste)
3 tablespoons Worcestershire sauce	

1. In a medium saucepan heat oil and garlic over medium heat for 1 minute. Add onion and cook for 10 minutes, until onion is soft and translucent.
2. Add the remaining ingredients, stir well, and simmer for 20 minutes over low heat. Remove from heat and blenderize to smooth and blend flavors. Cool, cover, and refrigerate. Keeps for 2 weeks.

Serves Twelve (2 tablespoons)

PER SERVING

Calories 25
Carbohydrate 5 grams
Protein 1 gram

Fat .5 grams (0 saturated)
Fiber .5 grams
Sodium 105 milligrams

Diabetic exchange = ½ Carbohydrate (for up to 3 tablespoons)
WW point comparison = 0 points

Tomato paste is rich in lycopene, a powerful antioxidant that may be beneficial in fighting certain forms of cancer and heart disease.

QUICK SMOOTH BARBECUE DIPPING SAUCE

Easy to make, and kids love it. It's great on anything you would use a barbecue sauce on, like barbecued chicken or ribs.

1	8-ounce can tomato sauce	4	tablespoons Splenda Granular
2	tablespoons water		
1	tablespoon Worcestershire sauce	1	teaspoon honey
			Pinch onion powder
1	tablespoon cider vinegar		Pinch salt

1. Place all ingredients in a small saucepan, stir, and cook for 5 minutes over low heat. (For a thicker sauce cook additional 5 minutes.)

Serves Six (2 tablespoons)

PER SERVING

Calories 15
Carbohydrate 4 grams
Protein 0.5 grams

Fat 0 grams (0 saturated)
Fiber .5 grams
Sodium 210 milligrams

Diabetic exchange = free exchange
WW point comparison = 0 points

One packet of Wendy's barbecue sauce contains 45 calories and 10 grams of carbohydrate—use two and that's 90 calories and 20 grams carb!

THAI PEANUT SAUCE

Peanut (satay) sauces are as common in Asia as barbecue sauce is here. In my version, I have eliminated the excess fat and, of course, the sugar. What I have not eliminated, although it does contain a bit of sugar, is the hoisin sauce. Hoisin sauce provides a rich flavor that no other ingredient can duplicate. You can find jars of it in the oriental section of your supermarket.

2 tablespoons light soy sauce	½ cup water
3 tablespoons natural rice vinegar	Pinch red pepper flakes
2 tablespoons hoisin sauce	3 tablespoons smooth peanut butter
2 tablespoons Splenda Granular	½ teaspoon cornstarch dissolved in 1 teaspoon water
1 teaspoon sesame oil	

1. Whisk all ingredients except peanut butter and cornstarch mixture together in a small saucepan. Add peanut butter and place over low heat. Heat, stirring with a whisk until smooth.
2. Bring to a low boil and add cornstarch mixture. Stir until sauce thickens and clears.

Serves Eight (2 tablespoons)

PER SERVING

Calories 55
Carbohydrate 4 grams
Protein 2 grams

Fat 4 grams (1 saturated)
Fiber 0 grams
Sodium 220 milligrams

Diabetic exchange = 1 Fat
WW point comparison = 1 point

This sauce is used for the satay on page 170. I also use it as a stir-fry sauce or toss it with pasta, chicken, and vegetables for a healthy oriental noodle bowl.

SWEET HORSERADISH SAUCE

I still remember my brother raving about a sandwich sauce called Horsey Sauce. It is a sweetened mayonnaise concoction flavored with horseradish, and it definitely gives great zip to sandwiches such as roast beef. In my own version, I use a technique I teach to chefs of substituting cottage cheese for mayonnaise.

½ **cup low-fat cottage cheese**	2 **tablespoons horseradish**
3 **tablespoons light sour cream**	1 **tablespoon Splenda Granular**

1. Place cottage cheese in food processor or blender and puree until completely smooth (like mayonnaise). Add sour cream, horseradish, and Splenda and blend again. Cover and refrigerate.

Serves Twelve (1 tablespoon)

PER SERVING

Calories 15
Carbohydrate 1 gram
Protein 1 gram

Fat 1 gram (1 saturated)
Fiber 0 grams
Sodium 45 milligrams

Diabetic exchange = free exchange
WW point comparison = 0 points

You may substitute pureed low-fat cottage cheese in any spread, dip, or dressing recipes for part or all of the mayonnaise or sour cream.

SWEET MUSTARD SAUCE AND DIP

This recipe is similar to the honey mustard sauce found at T.G.I. Friday's restaurant. I've used reduced-fat products and Splenda to cut the calories, fat, and carbohydrate by half. You can thin this sauce with a few tablespoons of hot water and use it as a sweet mustard salad dressing.

¼ cup reduced-fat mayonnaise (not nonfat)	1 tablespoon hot water
¼ cup light sour cream	1 tablespoon + 1 teaspoon Dijon mustard
2 tablespoons Splenda Granular	1½ teaspoons vinegar
	2 teaspoons honey

1. Place all ingredients in small bowl and whisk together. Cover and refrigerate to thicken. If you wish to use immediately as a sandwich spread, eliminate the hot water.

Serves Ten (1 tablespoon)

PER SERVING

Calories 35
Carbohydrate 2 grams
Protein 0 grams

Fat 2.5 grams (1 saturated)
Fiber 0 grams
Sodium 70 milligrams

Diabetic exchange = ½ Fat
WW point comparison = 1 point

Regular mayonnaise contains no carbohydrates but is a huge calorie splurge at 100 calories per tablespoon.

TERIYAKI SAUCE

I love teriyaki sauce because it is so versatile and tastes great as a marinade for all types and cuts of beef, pork, chicken, and seafood; as a dipping sauce for cooked meats; and as a stir-fry sauce if thickened with a touch of cornstarch.

⅓ cup light soy sauce	1 tablespoon brown sugar
¼ cup dry sherry	2 teaspoons sesame oil
2 tablespoons natural rice vinegar	1 teaspoon fresh grated ginger
3 tablespoons Splenda Granular	½ teaspoon minced garlic

1. Whisk all ingredients together in a small bowl. Store covered in the refrigerator.

Serves Ten (1 tablespoon)

PER SERVING

Calories 20
Carbohydrate 2 grams
Protein 1 gram

Fat 1 gram (0 saturated)
Fiber 0 grams
Sodium 260 milligrams

Diabetic exchange = free exchange
WW point comparison = 0 points

Natural rice vinegar contains no sugar. Seasoned rice vinegar is rice vinegar seasoned with sugar. Each tablespoon of vinegar contains about 1 teaspoon of sugar.

SPICY TERIYAKI SAUCE

Instead of ginger, this sauce uses more garlic and red pepper flakes to add some heat. I especially like to use this teriyaki sauce as a stir-fry sauce.

⅓ cup light soy sauce

¼ cup dry sherry

2 tablespoons natural rice vinegar

3 tablespoons Splenda Granular

1 tablespoon brown sugar

1 tablespoon sesame oil

1 teaspoon minced garlic

⅛ teaspoon red pepper flakes

1. Whisk all ingredients together in a small bowl. Store covered in the refrigerator.

Serves Ten (1 tablespoon)

PER SERVING

Calories 25
Carbohydrate 2 grams
Protein 1 gram

Fat 1.5 grams (0 saturated)
Fiber 0 grams
Sodium 260 milligrams

Diabetic exchange = free exchange
WW point comparison = 0 points

 After marinating meat, boil the leftover marinade and reduce the volume by one-half to use as a glaze on the cooked meat.

TWO-WAY CRANBERRY SAUCE

The thing I've come to realize about holiday cooking is that no one accepts a new dish (healthy or not) if it doesn't compare favorably to a traditional recipe. I guarantee that with this recipe no one will know you have taken out over 75 percent of the sugar that is needed to make a traditional cranberry sauce recipe, because this one tastes exactly the same! You may choose to leave the berries whole as I do, or strain the sauce to make a jellied cranberry sauce by selecting the variation below.

¼ **cup orange juice**
1 **teaspoon unflavored gelatin**
12 **ounces fresh cranberries, washed and picked over**
1 **cup water**

¾ **cup Splenda Granular**
3 **tablespoons granulated sugar**
Red food color (optional)

1. Place orange juice into a small bowl. Add gelatin. Let set 3 minutes.
2. Combine cranberries, water, Splenda, and sugar in a medium skillet. Bring to a boil. Add softened gelatin and simmer for 10 minutes or until most of the cranberries pop open. Adjust color by adding 2–3 drops of red food color if desired.

JELLIED VARIATION: Increase gelatin to 2 teaspoons. Strain sauce by pressing berries and juice through sieve with the back of a spoon. Refrigerate sauce overnight.

Serves Ten (¼ cup whole or 2 tablespoons jellied)

PER SERVING

Calories 30
Carbohydrate 8 grams
Protein 1 gram

Fat 0 grams (0 saturated)
Fiber 2 grams
Sodium 0 milligrams

Diabetic exchange = ½ Fruit
WW points Comparison = 1 point

Traditional cranberry sauce can have up to 45 grams of carbohydrate in a ¼-cup serving.

SENSATIONAL NO-COOK CRANBERRY RELISH

Cranberry relishes have become increasingly popular. In this tart and refreshing version I have included a few added touches that really make it stand out. Prepare it at least one day ahead of time to allow the flavors to meld.

1 12-ounce bag cranberries, washed and picked over	2 tablespoons brown sugar
	2 tablespoons orange liqueur
1 orange, peeled and seeded (reserve ¼ of rind)	¾ cup Splenda Granular

1. Place ½ the cranberries, the orange and the orange peel in a food processor and pulse until mixture is finely chopped (not pureed). Pour into a large bowl. Repeat process with second half of cranberries and brown sugar. Add to bowl.
2. Stir orange liqueur and Splenda into cranberry mixture. Cover and refrigerate overnight or longer before serving (holds well up to 2 weeks).

Serves Eight

PER SERVING

Calories 35
Carbohydrate 7 grams
Protein 0 grams

Fat 0 grams (0 saturated)
Fiber 1 gram
Sodium 0 milligrams

Diabetic exchange = ½ Fruit
WW point comparison = 1 point

Cranberries (originally called crane berries) are full of antioxidants and vitamin C.

CRANBERRY CHUTNEY

Every year I make cranberry chutney during the holidays to serve with turkey. Chutneys combine vinegar with sugar for a balance of sweet and sour flavors, but this one also has a touch of heat from red pepper flakes, along with a lovely hint of orange. Make another batch or use leftover chutney as a great spread for cold turkey sandwiches. This chutney also goes well served with pork tenderloin.

- 1 teaspoon canola oil
- 1 large shallot, finely chopped (⅓ cup)
- 1 12-ounce package cranberries
- ½ cup Splenda Granular
- ½ cup orange juice
- ⅓ cup cider vinegar
- 1 tablespoon brown sugar
- ½ teaspoon ground ginger
- Scant ¼ teaspoon red pepper flakes
- 1 tablespoon orange zest

1. In a large saucepan heat oil and sauté shallot 3–4 minutes or until softened. Add all remaining ingredients except zest and bring to a boil. Lower heat and simmer for 15 minutes, stirring occasionally. Add zest and cook 15 more minutes or until thickened. Cool and store in refrigerator. Serve cool or room temperature.

Serves Twelve (2 tablespoons)

PER SERVING

Calories 35
Carbohydrate 8 grams
Protein 0 grams

Fat 0 grams (0 saturated)
Fiber 1 gram
Sodium 0 milligrams

Diabetic exchange = ½ Fruit
WW point comparison = 1 point

I usually add a couple of drops of red food color to give a deep red color to the chutney, especially if I spoon it into jars to give as gifts during the holidays.

PEACH CHUTNEY

My next-door neighbor is a gracious recipient of many of my recipe trials. She was delighted on the day she received a container of this scrumptious Peach Chutney. In fact, she mentioned it for weeks! It makes a wonderful accompaniment for grilled meat or fish. For an interesting flavor twist, try the Southwestern variation.

6 fresh medium peaches (1½ pounds)	**⅓** cup cider vinegar
1 tablespoon lemon juice	**1** teaspoon fresh grated ginger
½ cup chopped onion	**2** teaspoons honey
½ cup chopped red pepper	**⅛** teaspoon cinnamon
1 teaspoon oil	**⅛** teaspoon red pepper flakes
½ cup Splenda Granular	

1. Plunge peaches into boiling water for one minute. Immediately drop into cold water and cool. Peel, pit, and chop into medium-sized pieces (about 3 cups). Sprinkle with lemon juice.
2. In a medium saucepan sauté onion and pepper in oil until slightly softened. Add peaches and remaining ingredients and bring to low boil. Reduce heat to simmer and cook for 30 minutes, stirring occasionally until cooked down and thickened.

SOUTHWESTERN VARIATION: Substitute ⅛ teaspoon turmeric for cinnamon and add ½ teaspoon cumin. Use one finely diced jalapeno pepper instead of red pepper flakes and lime juice for the lemon juice.

Serves Eight (¼ cup)

PER SERVING

Calories 45	Fat 0 grams (0 saturated)
Carbohydrate 11 grams	Fiber 2 grams
Protein 1 gram	Sodium 0 milligrams

Diabetic exchange = 1 Fruit
WW point comparison = 1 point

Chutneys can be made from many different types of fruits and vegetables. They can be made fresh like this one or canned like jelly. Fresh chutneys can be kept in the refrigerator for up to one month.

TOMATO GINGER JAM

Several years ago I attended a "Holiday Gifts" class at a local cooking school where I learned to make a delectable chutneylike jam with tomatoes and ginger similar to those found at upscale gourmet markets. This version retains the flavor and tangy quality of the original without the copius sugar. Use it on grilled meats or as a topping for crackers spread with light cream cheese for a delicious and festive-looking treat.

1	28-ounce can plum or diced tomatoes	1	teaspoon minced garlic
⅔	cup Splenda Granular	½	teaspoon salt
⅔	cup cider vinegar	⅛	teaspoon cayenne pepper or ¼ teaspoon red pepper flakes
2	tablespoons corn syrup		
1¼	teaspoons ground ginger		

1. Combine all ingredients in a heavy saucepan. Bring to a boil over high heat; then lower heat and simmer, stirring occasionally, until liquid evaporates and jam thickens, about 1 hour. Cool, cover, and store in refrigerator. Keeps for up to 1 month.

Serves Ten (3 tablespoons)

PER SERVING

Calories 35
Carbohydrate 8 grams
Protein 1 gram

Fat 0 grams (0 saturated)
Fiber 2 grams
Sodium 0 milligrams

Diabetic exchange = 1 Vegetable
WW point comparison = 1 point

LOW-SUGAR STRAWBERRY FREEZER JAM

An award-winning strawberry jam recipe I found on the Internet called for 5 cups of crushed strawberries and 7 cups of sugar! This recipe uses a fraction of the sugar—a mere ⅓ cup—to make 4 cups of jam. You can omit it altogether, but granulated sugar helps to add clarity and improves the overall quality of the jam. Be sure to use "no-sugar needed" pectin in order for the jam to jell.

2 quarts fresh strawberries, washed and stemmed (4 cups crushed)

1 1¾-ounce package no-sugar-needed pectin

2½ cups Splenda Granular

⅓ cup granulated sugar

3-4 drops red food coloring

1. Mix crushed berries and pectin together in a large saucepan. Stir and let stand 10 minutes. Turn heat to medium, add Splenda and sugar and cook until mixture comes to a boil. Cook for one minute. Stir in desired amount of food coloring and skim foam off top.
2. Place in containers and refrigerate (to be eaten within one month) or freeze (for up to one year).

Serves Forty-eight (1 tablespoon)

PER SERVING

Calories 15
Carbohydrate 4 grams
Protein 0 grams

Fat 0 grams (0 saturated)
Fiber .5 grams
Sodium 0 milligrams

Diabetic exchange = free exchange
WW point comparison = 0 points

If the powdered pectin has hardened, blenderize to turn it back into a powder.

MICROWAVE CINNAMON APPLESAUCE

Fresh applesauce, especially served chunky, makes a great side dish. This recipe tastes like the old-fashioned kind but it is made with a very modern appliance—the microwave.

6 medium apples (1½ pounds), peeled, halved and cored	1 tablespoon lemon juice
	½ cup Splenda Granular
	½ teaspoon cinnamon
⅔ cup water	1 tablespoon brown sugar

1. Cut apples into either thick slices or 1-inch chunks. Place apples in a deep, microwave-safe casserole dish. Add water, lemon juice, Splenda, and cinnamon to apples.
2. Cook, uncovered, on high for 5 minutes. Stir, mashing apples into the liquid.
3. Cook for an additional 5–8 minutes or until apples are tender. Mash apples again, mixing with liquid, until desired texture. Stir brown sugar into hot apple mixture. Serve hot or cool and store in refrigerator until ready to use. Keeps about 3–4 days.

Serves Six (½ cup)

PER SERVING

Calories 70	Fat 0 grams (0 saturated)
Carbohydrate 18 grams	Fiber 2 grams
Protein 0 grams	Sodium 0 milligrams

Diabetic exchange = 1 Fruit
WW point comparison = 1 point

TIP For the best applesauce, mix a couple of kinds of apples together—like Gravenstein or Pippin blended with Macintosh or Golden Delicious.

BREAD AND BUTTER PICKLES

I was delighted with the outcome of these pickles as they taste even better than the commercial brands that are loaded with sugar. Small pickling cukes or gherkins are ideal, but regular salad cucumbers work just fine.

1 ½ pounds of cucumbers, ends trimmed and sliced (unpeeled)

1 medium onion, thinly sliced

1 tablespoon pickling salt

1 ½ cups vinegar

1 cup Splenda Granular

1 ½ teaspoons mustard seed

1 teaspoon cornstarch

¾ teaspoon tumeric

½ teaspoon celery seed

1. Place cucumbers and onion in a large bowl and toss with pickling salt. Cover and refrigerate for 1–2 hours. Rinse well in colander under running water, drain, and place in large bowl.
2. In a medium pot, combine the remaining ingredients and bring to boil over high heat. Stir until slightly thickened and clear. Pour hot marinade over cucumbers and onions. Cool to room temperature, cover, and refrigerate. Keeps up to 1 month.

PICKLED MIXED VEGETABLES VARIATION: Marinate up to 5 cups mixed blanched carrots, peppers, cauliflower, and onion in place of cucumbers and onion. Add a touch of crushed red pepper for zing.

Serves Ten (½ cup)

PER SERVING

Calories 20
Carbohydrate 5 grams
Protein 0 grams

Fat 0 grams (0 saturated)
Fiber .5 grams
Sodium 120 milligrams

Diabetic exchange = 1 Vegetable
WW point comparison = 0 points

These sweet and crunchy pickles can really satisfy a sweet tooth.

Protein-Packed Entrées

PROTEIN IS KING—AT LEAST THE KING OF THE MAJOR NUTRIENTS IF YOU look at today's popular diets. And while all of the hype may not be true, protein is definitely an important nutrient. In fact, new scientific findings suggest that eating more high quality protein can help a person maintain muscle mass and reduce body fat while dieting. Exactly what we all want to do when we lose weight! Protein is also necessary to maintain everything from your skin to your immune system to your muscles. Additionally, protein fills you up (it has great satiety value), can provide you with energy, and does not raise insulin or blood sugar levels (unless, of course, you coat it with sugar).

Healthy, high-quality protein is characterized by having a complete complement of amino acids, like those found in chicken, beef, pork, seafood, eggs, and dairy, and is not full of fat or fillers. When I think of solid sources of healthy protein, I think of lean yet tender and delicious entrées—entrées that provide me with substantial satisfaction without the high price of extra fat or unnecessary sugar. All of the recipes in this chapter fit that bill. I use only lean meats and have eliminated the sugar (but not the great sweet taste). I have included once taboo, but oh so satisfying, foods like Sloppy Joes and Barbecued Pork Sandwiches. You will also find great entertaining fare, like cocktail meatballs and grilled salmon, as well as many of today's global taste favorites, like Sweet and Sour Chicken, Spicy Orange Beef, and Shrimp Satay. For me, these delicious entrées definitely rule!

PROTEIN-PACKED ENTRÉES

Sloppy Joes

Barbecued Pork Sandwiches

Caribbean Chicken

Simple Southwest Salmon

Maple Glazed Ham Steaks

Bourbon Chicken

Spicy Orange Beef

Shrimp Satay with Thai Peanut Sauce

Sweet and Sour Chicken

Baked Fish with Oriental Pesto

Asian Barbecued Pork Tenderloin

Grilled Salmon with Mustard Dill Sauce

Zesty Chicken Strips with Sweet Mustard Dip

Cocktail Meatballs with Quick Sweet and Sour Sauce

SLOPPY JOES

Sloppy Joes are thought to have been created during World War II as a way to extend precious beef rations. Always messy, these simple-to-make hearty Joes, made with lean ground sirloin, make a hearty, healthy meal.

1	pound lean ground sirloin	1	tablespoon vinegar
1	small onion, diced	1	tablespoon Worcestershire sauce
1	green pepper, diced		
4	stalks celery, diced	½	teaspoon chili powder
1	cup water	½	teaspoon paprika
1	6-ounce can tomato paste		Pinch of salt
3	tablespoons Splenda Granular	6	light wheat buns

1. In a medium skillet, over medium heat, brown beef, onion, green pepper, and celery.
2. Add remaining ingredients, except buns; mix thoroughly. Reduce heat, and simmer for 20–30 minutes.
3. Serve scant ½ cup on each bun.

Serves Six

PER SERVING

Calories 290
Carbohydrate 26 grams
Protein 20 grams

Fat 12 grams (5 saturated)
Fiber 4 grams
Sodium 500 milligrams

Diabetic exchange = 1½ Carbohydrate, 3 Lean Meat, 1 Fat
WW point comparison = 6 points

Worcestershire sauce is actually quite exotic. It contains not only anchovies but tamarinds, molasses, vinegar, garlic, cloves, chilies, onions, and sometimes fruit.

BARBECUED PORK SANDWICHES

Soft, shredded pork smothered in sweet tangy barbecue sauce, all served up on a bun for less than 250 calories. This recipe yields a dozen sandwiches, making it perfect for entertaining. The Sweet and Sour Party Slaw (page 110) makes a great low-carbohydrate accompaniment.

2–2¼ pounds boneless pork loin roast, trimmed of excess fat

1 8-ounce can tomato sauce

1 6-ounce can tomato paste

¼ cup vinegar

½ cup Splenda Granular

2 tablespoons molasses

2 tablespoons Worcestershire sauce

2 teaspoons onion powder

12 light wheat hamburger buns

1. Place roast in a 4-quart Dutch oven or large pot; add 2 cups water. Cover and cook for 2½ hours or until meat shreds when tested with fork. Remove meat from liquid and pull apart with fork; set aside.
2. Drain cooking liquid, reserving 1 cup, and skim fat. Return 1 cup of liquid to pot. Add remaining ingredients (except buns) to pot and stir. Gently add meat to sauce (overstirring will turn meat to mush). Cover and simmer on low for 30 minutes.
3. Scoop ¼ cup barbecue pork onto each bun and serve.

Serves Twelve

PER SERVING

Calories 245
Carbohydrate 27 grams
Protein 21 grams

Fat 7 grams (2 saturated)
Fiber 4 grams
Sodium 510 milligrams

Diabetic exchange = 1½ Carbohydrate, 3 Lean Meat
WW point comparison = 5 points

The light wheat buns I use contain 85 calories, 18 grams of carbohydrate, and 3 grams of fiber per bun.

CARIBBEAN CHICKEN

This tropics-inspired dish brings back pleasing memories of time spent in the Caribbean. The piquant sauce has a fresh citrus taste that is both sweet and savory.

SAUCE

- ¼ cup unsweetened pineapple juice
- 2 tablespoons lime juice
- 3 tablespoons Splenda Granular
- 2 tablespoons low-sugar peach jam
- 1 tablespoon light soy sauce
- ½ teaspoon crushed dry thyme leaves
- ¼ teaspoon powdered ginger
- ¼ teaspoon nutmeg
- 3-4 drops Tabasco
- 4 5-ounce skinless, boneless chicken breasts

1. In a small bowl whisk together all ingredients except chicken.
2. Pound chicken between sheets of plastic wrap or wax paper to ¼-inch thickness. Place in shallow dish and cover with sauce. Marinate one hour (or longer).
3. Heat grill or broiler. Remove chicken from sauce. Pour sauce into a small saucepan. Place over medium heat and bring to a low boil. Turn down and simmer.
4. Grill or broil chicken 4–5 minutes per side or until juices run clear. Spoon sauce over chicken and serve.

Serves 4 per serving

PER SERVING

Calories 240
Carbohydrate 8 grams
Protein 31 grams

Fat 8 grams (2.5 saturated)
Fiber 0 grams
Sodium 240 milligrams

Diabetic exchange = 4 Lean Meat, ½ Carbohydrate
WW point comparison = 5 points

The enzyme bromelain found in pineapple juice is a powerful tenderizer, making it an excellent addition to marinades.

SIMPLE SOUTHWEST SALMON

This dish may be simple to make but the flavor is anything but. Sweet, spicy, and savory, it will definitely perk up your taste buds. Leftovers are terrific, too.

4 **5-ounce salmon fillets**	2 **teaspoons chili powder**
2 **tablespoons pineapple juice**	¾ **teaspoon ground cumin**
1 **tablespoon lime or lemon juice**	¼ **teaspoon salt**
	⅛ **teaspoon cinnamon**
3 **tablespoons Splenda Granular**	

1. Place salmon in shallow dish. Pour pineapple and lemon juice over salmon, cover, and place in refrigerator for 30 minutes.
2. Preheat oven to 400°F. In a small bowl combine remaining ingredients. Remove salmon from marinade. Pat spice mixture onto fillets. Place fillets on baking pan and cook for 15–20 minutes or until fish flakes easily when tested with a fork. Serve hot or, alternatively, at room temperature.

Serves Four

PER SERVING

Calories 225*
Carbohydrate 2 grams
Protein 28 grams

Fat 12 grams (1.5 saturated)
Fiber 0 grams
Sodium 220 milligrams

Diabetic exchange = 4 Lean Meat
WW point comparison = 5 points

*Average of wild and farm-raised salmon

Did you know: Wild salmon can have up to 6 grams less fat in a 5-ounce portion, compared with farm-raised salmon.

MAPLE GLAZED HAM STEAKS

While whole hams are usually reserved for special occasions and entertaining, lean ham steaks provide a quick and tasty anyday supper. This unusual glaze uses sugar-free maple syrup as its base. Choose one that contains Splenda.

SAUCE

1/3 cup sugar-free maple syrup

2 tablespoons unsweetened applesauce

2 tablespoons Splenda Granular

1 tablespoon ketchup

1 teaspoon Dijon mustard

1/2 teaspoon salt

Pinch of garlic powder

2 fully cooked 3/4 - to 1-inch-thick lean ham steaks (12 ounces each)

1. In a small saucepan over medium heat whisk together all sauce ingredients. Cook for 5 minutes over low heat.
2. Place ham steaks on baking sheet. Spoon one-half of sauce over steaks. Broil (2 inches from heating element) for 5 minutes. Turn steaks, spoon on remaining sauce, and broil for 5 minutes more or until steaks are heated throughout.

Serves Four

PER SERVING

Calories 230
Carbohydrate 9 grams
Protein 33 grams

Fat 8 grams (2 saturated)
Fiber 0 grams
Sodium 1,980 milligrams

Diabetic exchange = 5 Lean Meat
WW point comparison = 5 points

Because ham is cured, it is naturally high in sodium. If you are on a sodium-restricted diet, look for a reduced-salt ham.

BOURBON CHICKEN

Whenever I take my boys to the shopping mall, they head straight for the food court looking for a sample of a dish named bourbon chicken. It doesn't actually contain alcohol, but this delicious version does.

⅓ cup light soy sauce	1 teaspoon molasses
⅓ cup Splenda Granular	1 teaspoon powdered ginger
⅓ cup bourbon whiskey	½ teaspoon garlic powder
2 tablespoons dried, minced onion	1 pound boneless chicken tenderloins

1. In a large bowl combine all ingredients except chicken and stir to mix. Add chicken and stir to coat. Cover and refrigerate for several hours or overnight.
2. Preheat oven to 350°F. Place chicken and marinade in baking dish. Bake for 30 minutes, basting occasionally with marinade.
3. Remove from oven. Baste chicken with remaining marinade and serve.

Serves Four

PER SERVING

Calories 180
Carbohydrate 3 grams
Protein 23 grams

Fat 2.5 grams (1 saturated)
Fiber 0 grams
Sodium 1,060 milligrams

Diabetic exchange = 4 Very Lean Meat
WW point comparison = 3 points

SPICY ORANGE BEEF

Stir-frying rather than deep-frying the beef in this popular dish cuts the fat but not the flavor. The sweet and spicy orange sauce is what really makes the dish.

1 pound top sirloin or flank steak, partially frozen	2 teaspoons vinegar
2 tablespoons sherry	1 teaspoon sesame oil
2 tablespoons light soy sauce	1/2 teaspoon red pepper flakes (1/4 if you don't like spicy)
1 tablespoon cornstarch	
	1 tablespoon canola or peanut oil
SAUCE	
1 teaspoon cornstarch	1 medium onion, cut into 1/2-inch dice
1/4 cup orange juice	
3 tablespoons Splenda Granular	2 small yellow peppers, cut into strips
2 tablespoons light soy sauce	1 cup sliced water chestnuts
2 tablespoons low-sugar orange marmalade	2 green onions, chopped (white and green)

1. Slice steak thinly across the grain. Place in medium bowl, add sherry, soy sauce, and cornstarch and toss to coat meat. Set aside.
2. Combine sauce ingredients in a small bowl. Set aside.
3. Heat wok until hot. Add oil. When oil is very hot, add beef. (It should sizzle as it hits wok.) Stir-fry for 3–4 minutes until no longer pink. Remove from wok. Add onion to wok and stir 1 minute. Add peppers and water chestnuts. Stir-fry additional 2–3 minutes. Add sauce mixture, stir well. Add beef to hot sauce. Toss in green onions. Stir just until beef is coated and serve.

Serves Four

PER SERVING

Calories 310
Carbohydrate 16 grams
Protein 27 grams

Fat 15 grams (3.5 saturated)
Fiber 2 grams
Sodium 610 milligrams

Diabetic exchange = 1 Vegetable, 4 Lean Meat, ½ Carbohydrate, ½ Fat
WW point comparison = 7 points

Slicing the meat while it is slightly frozen makes it easy to cut very thin, uniform slices for stir-frying.

SHRIMP SATAY WITH THAI PEANUT SAUCE

Widely cooked throughout Asia, sate, or satay, is marinated meat, fish, or fowl threaded onto wooden or bamboo skewers. These tasty shrimp satay sticks served with Thai Peanut Sauce are universally welcomed.

8 bamboo or wooden skewers

1 tablespoon olive oil

1 tablespoon lime juice

1 tablespoon each light soy sauce and sherry

1 tablespoon Splenda Granular

2 cloves garlic. minced

1½ pounds large to extra-large shrimp (21–26 count), peeled and deveined

Thai Peanut Sauce (page 146)

1. Presoak bamboo or wooden skewers in cold water for 30–60 minutes to prevent burning.
2. Mix together all ingredients (except Thai Peanut Sauce) in a large bowl and add shrimp. Refrigerate and marinate for 30 minutes (or longer). Thread shrimp (to lie flat) onto skewers.
3. Cook shrimp on hot grill or place 4–6 inches under broiler for 4–6 minutes, turning once.
4. Serve with Thai Peanut Sauce.

Serves Four (1 stick plus 2 tablespoons Thai Peanut Sauce)

PER SERVING

Calories 175
Carbohydrate 4 grams
Protein 24 grams

Fat 3.5 grams (0.5 saturated)
Fiber 0 grams
Sodium 450 milligrams

Diabetic exchange = 3 Lean Meat
WW point comparison = 4 points

Chicken breast can be substituted for the shrimp. One pound of boneless, skinless breast will yield approximately 8 skewers.

SWEET AND SOUR CHICKEN

When you think of entrées with lots of sugar, traditional Asian sweet and sour dishes certainly come to mind. I didn't have to look far for a model for this recipe, as my mom always made great sweet and sour chicken. I am thrilled to tell you that my Splenda version is indistinguishable from hers. Thanks, Mom.

1 **pound boneless, skinless chicken breast, cut into bite-size pieces**	½ **cup green pepper, cut in 1-inch pieces**
2 **teaspoons cornstarch**	½ **cup pineapple chunks, well drained**
1 **tablespoon sherry**	½ **cup Splenda Granular**
½ **teaspoon salt**	¼ **cup ketchup**
½ **teaspoon grated ginger (optional)**	1 **tablespoon light soy sauce**
SAUCE	⅓ **cup cider vinegar**
½ **cup peeled carrots, cut in ¼ inch slices**	2 **tablespoons cornstarch + ¼ cup water**

1. In medium bowl combine chicken, cornstarch, sherry, salt, and ginger. Toss to coat meat and set aside.
2. Put carrots in small saucepan with ½ cup water. Bring to boil. Boil for 1 minute. Add green pepper and boil for 1 more minute. Drain vegetables and rinse thoroughly in cold water. Add pineapple and set mixture aside.
3. In a small saucepan, combine Splenda, ketchup, soy sauce, and vinegar. Bring to low simmer, add cornstarch mixture, and cook, stirring, until thickened and clear. Stir in vegetables.
4. Heat wok until hot. Add oil. When oil is very hot, add chicken. (It should sizzle as it hits wok.) Stir-fry for 2–3 minutes until no longer pink. Remove from wok.
5. Combine sweet and sour sauce with chicken. Serve over brown or white rice if desired.

Serves Four

PER SERVING

Calories 210
Carbohydrate 17 grams
Protein 24 grams

Fat 5 grams (1 saturated)
Fiber 1 grams
Sodium 370 milligrams

Diabetic exchange = 4 Very Lean Meat, 1 Carbohydrate
WW point comparison = 4 points

One-half cup of cooked brown rice provides 110 calories and 22 grams carbohydrate. It also provides 2 grams fiber and 3 grams protein.

BAKED FISH WITH ORIENTAL PESTO

This Oriental Pesto, as I call it, truly is one of my favorite sauces. Over the years I have taught it in my cooking classes and served it to many guests in my home. Because you make more than you need, save the rest for the next day, when you can make it seem like a different meal by using chicken instead of fish.

2 tablespoons fresh lime juice
1 tablespoon light soy sauce
1 tablespoon sherry
1 teaspoon sesame oil
1 teaspoon Splenda Granular
4 5-ounce fish fillets (sea bass, halibut, salmon, or other preferred fish fillet)

PESTO

1 teaspoon canola oil
1 teaspoon garlic, minced
2 teaspoons fresh ginger, minced finely

3 tablespoons each fresh lemon juice, rice vinegar, and rice wine
2 tablespoons light soy sauce
2 tablespoons Splenda Granular
1/4 cup green onion (white and green), minced finely
1/4 cup fresh cilantro, minced finely
1 teaspoon cornstarch + 2 teaspoons cold water

1. Preheat grill or oven to 350°F.
2. In a small bowl, mix together the first 5 ingredients and pour over fish; set aside for 20–30 minutes to marinate.
3. Heat oil in a small saucepan until very hot; and add garlic and ginger. Heat for 20 seconds. Add remaining ingredients, except cornstarch mixture, and stir well. Bring sauce to simmer and stir in cornstarch mixture. Cook, stirring, until pesto thickens and clears.
4. To bake fish, cover fish with foil and bake for 20 minutes, or until fish flakes easily when tested with fork.
5. Serve fish draped with 2 tablespoons sauce (you will have sauce left over).

Serves Four

PER SERVING (*with sea bass or other white fish*)

Calories 190
Carbohydrate 2 grams
Protein 30 grams

Fat 6 grams (1 saturated)
Fiber 0 grams
Sodium 520 milligrams

Diabetic exchange = 4 Very Lean Meat, 1 Fat
WW point comparison = 4 points

ASIAN BARBECUED PORK TENDERLOIN

Hoisin is a thick, sweet, spicy condiment used extensively in Asian cuisine. In addition to being spread on pancakes for mu shu pork, it is used for delicious stir-fry or barbecue sauce like this one.

¼ cup orange juice	2 tablespoons hoisin sauce
3 tablespoons Splenda Granular	2 teaspoons sesame oil
	½ teaspoon grated ginger
2 tablespoons light soy sauce	1¼ pounds pork tenderloin

1. In a small bowl combine all ingredients except pork.
2. Place pork in shallow dish and coat with sauce. Cover and marinate for several hours or overnight.
3. Preheat oven to 425°F. Remove pork from sauce and place on baking sheet covered with foil. Coat with marinade and cook for 20 minutes or until internal temperature reaches 145–150°F. Slice thin across grain and serve.

Serves Four

PER SERVING

Calories 210
Carbohydrate 5 grams
Protein 30 grams

Fat 7 grams (2 saturated)
Fiber 0 grams
Sodium 490 milligrams

Diabetic exchange = 4 Very Lean Meat, ½ Carbohydrate
WW point comparison = 5 points

Hoisin is made from soybeans, chilies, garlic, ginger, and sugar. Brands vary quite a bit from one to another. It should be very dark and have a complex flavor. Koon Chun is one preferred brand.

GRILLED SALMON WITH MUSTARD DILL SAUCE

This dill sauce is a real winner. It's equally delicious served with gravlax (cold cured, smoked salmon) or over grilled salmon fillets. If you'd like to create your own signature dish, simply substitute your favorite fish.

3 tablespoons creamy Dijon mustard (like Dijonnaise)	1 tablespoon minced fresh dill
2 tablespoons Splenda Granular	½ teaspoon dry mustard
	3 tablespoons virgin olive oil
1½ tablespoons white wine vinegar	Fresh pepper to taste
	4 salmon fillets (4–5 ounces each)

1. In a small bowl whisk together the first 5 ingredients. Continue to whisk while drizzling in olive oil 1 tablespoon at a time. Add pepper to taste.

2. Grill salmon over high heat, cooking each side approximately 5 minutes (for 1-inch fillets), or until fish flakes apart easily when teased with a fork. Place fillets onto plates or serving tray and spoon sauce over top.

Serves Four

PER SERVING

Calories 285
Carbohydrate 2 grams
Protein 24 grams

Fat 19 grams (2 saturated)
Fiber 0 grams
Sodium 310 milligrams

Diabetic exchange = 4 Lean Meat, 1½ Fat
WW point comparison = 7 points

This is a lovely dish to serve guests. Be sure to garnish with additional fresh dill and lemon slices. If you are really watching the fat (or WW points) you can save an additional 6 grams of fat and 50 calories (2 points' worth) by switching to a white fish, like snapper or cod.

ZESTY CHICKEN STRIPS WITH SWEET MUSTARD DIP

Whether served as an appetizer or an entrée, chicken strips are a definite crowd-pleaser. I serve them here as an entrée with a dipping sauce patterned after the honey mustard sauces found at most restaurants.

1 pound boneless chicken breast or tenders	½ teaspoon garlic powder
1 large egg white	½ teaspoon each crushed thyme, oregano, and basil leaves
1 teaspoon Dijon mustard	
½ cup plain bread crumbs	Black pepper to taste
4 tablespoons cornmeal	Sweet Mustard Dip (page 148)
4 tablespoons grated Parmesan cheese	

1. Preheat oven to 450°F. Coat baking sheet with nonstick cooking spray. Place baking sheet in oven to preheat.
2. Pound chicken breasts to flatten slightly. Slice into ½-inch strips. In a small bowl beat egg white and mustard. Coat strips.
3. In a medium bowl stir together remaining ingredients, except Sweet Mustard Dip. Thoroughly coat each piece of chicken with breadcrumbs. When all pieces are coated, remove prepared pan from oven and lay fingers on hot baking sheet.
4. Bake 8 minutes, turn, and bake an additional 7 minutes until brown and crisp.
5. While baking, prepare Sweet Mustard Dip (page 00). Serve strips with dip.

Serves Four

PER SERVING

Calories 280
Carbohydrate 15 grams
Protein 27 grams

Fat 11 grams (3 saturated)
Fiber 1 gram
Sodium 300 milligrams

Diabetic exchange = 4 Very Lean Meat, 1½ Fat, 1 Carbohydrate
WW point comparison = 6 points

COCKTAIL MEATBALLS WITH QUICK SWEET AND SOUR SAUCE

Make these for a party and watch them disappear. I've provided a recipe here for meatballs, but in a pinch you can buy prepared ones from your grocer's freezer. Be sure to check the labels, as they can be full of both fat and fillers.

1   pound prepared lean ground beef (or turkey) meatballs

or

MEATBALLS

½   pound lean ground beef (or turkey)

⅓   cup unseasoned bread crumbs

1   large egg

2   tablespoons dry minced onion

2   tablespoons fresh parsley, minced

½   teaspoon salt

¼   teaspoon pepper

½   cup 1% milk

SAUCE

⅓   cup ketchup

¼   cup cider vinegar

¼   cup Splenda Granular

2   teaspoons Worcestershire sauce

⅔   cup cold water

1   tablespoon + 1 teaspoon cornstarch

1. Preheat oven to 350°F. In a large bowl mix all ingredients for meatballs. Using hands, roll mixture into 1-inch balls and place onto ungreased baking sheet. Bake for 15 minutes or until center is no longer pink.
2. In small saucepan combine sauce ingredients. Place over medium heat and simmer until thickened and clear. Pour sauce over meatballs. Serve hot.

Serves Ten (3–4 meatballs plus sauce)

PER SERVING

Calories 130

Carbohydrate 9 grams

Protein 12 grams

Fat 5 grams (2 saturated)

Fiber 0 grams

Sodium 580 milligrams

Diabetic exchange = 2 Lean Meat, ½ Carbohydrate

WW point comparison = 3 points

How popular are cocktail-style meatballs? A recent Web search offered thousands of recipes to choose from!

Custards, Puddings, and Mousses . . . Oh My!

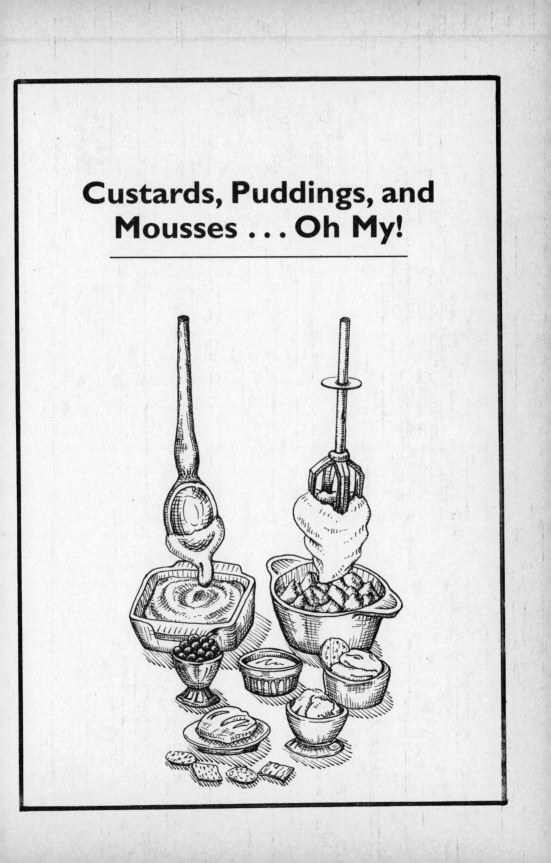

SPELL "STRESSED" BACKWARD AND WHAT DO YOU GET? "DESSERTS"—THE ultimate comfort food! It is fitting that I start the dessert chapters off with sweet and soothing custards, creamy puddings, and decadent mousses, since I can't think of another group of desserts that comfort any better. My goal in this chapter is to bring back all the comfort and tradition of these home-style treats without any of the modern guilt. I am happy to say my tasters have unanimously agreed that I succeeded! To start, the egg custards, high in protein and calcium, are now low in fat and sugar. They are excellent for dessert, a snack, or even for breakfast. In addition to Traditional Egg Custard, there are several variations from which to choose. I particularly enjoy the Coffee Custard for breakfast and the Eggnog Custard for holiday gatherings. If puddings are what soothe you, I have included one of my all-time soothing favorites: Fluffy Tapioca Pudding, along with New Orleans Bread Pudding and a couple of versions of lovely rice pudding. Since puddings are made with starches, they, like rice and bread, are higher in carbohydrate than other recipes in this book. Yet when compared to their traditional counterparts, you will see the carbs have been substantially reduced. The great part is that there is essentially no difference in taste. (The New Orleans Bread Pudding with Bourbon Sauce, for example, has *less than one-third* of the usual carbohydrates, fat, and calories of those bread puddings found in restaurants.)

And last but not least, if cool and creamy is what you seek, I've got you covered, too. From light-as-air Orange Snow to Dark Chocolate Mousse, there is something for everyone. So sit back, relax and simply enjoy.

CUSTARDS, PUDDINGS, AND MOUSSES . . . OH MY!

Traditional Egg Custard

Fabulous Custard Variations

Fluffy Tapioca Pudding

Creamy Rice Pudding

Baked Brown Rice Pudding

New Orleans Bread Pudding with Bourbon Sauce

Strawberry Fool

French Cream with Raspberry Sauce

Orange Snow

Pumpkin Mousse with Gingersnaps

Dark Chocolate Mousse

TRADITIONAL EGG CUSTARD

Custards can be made very rich (like crème brulée) to very lean (using only skim milk and egg whites). I've chosen to balance good taste with good nutrition in developing this traditional custard, by using reduced-fat milk and a combination of whole eggs and egg whites. Note, though, that as with traditional custard, straining the milk mixture and baking in a water bath are essential in giving this custard its proper texture.

2 large eggs	**1 cup evaporated low-fat or skim milk**
2 large egg whites	
⅔ cup Splenda Granular	**Freshly grated or ground nutmeg**
2 teaspoons vanilla	
2 cups 1% milk	

1. Preheat oven to 325°F. In a medium bowl whisk together eggs, egg whites, Splenda, and vanilla. Set aside.
2. In a small saucepan bring milks to a low simmer. Whisk a small amount of hot milk into egg mixture to temper eggs. Whisk in remaining milk. Strain mixture into a large measuring cup with pouring lip or bowl.
3. Pour or ladle mixture into six 6-ounce custard cups or ramekins. Sprinkle with nutmeg. Place cups in large baking dish and place in oven. Pour very hot water into baking dish until it reaches halfway up the sides of the custard cups. Bake custards 50–60 minutes or until edges are set and center jiggles slightly when shaken.

Serves Six (½ cup)

PER SERVING

Calories 110

Carbohydrate 11 grams

Protein 9 grams

Fat 3.5 grams (2 saturated)

Fiber 1 gram

Sodium 125 milligrams

Diabetic exchange = 1 Low-fat Milk

WW point comparison = 2 points

 If you are on a diet like The Zone, this is the perfect snack or dessert. Like a Balance Bar, the nutrient ratio is approximately 35 percent protein, 30 percent fat, and 40 percent carbohydrate.

FABULOUS CUSTARD VARIATIONS

If you like custard, you are sure to enjoy these delightful variations. Simply use the Traditional Egg Custard (page 80) as a base and make the changes as directed.

EXTRA CREAMY CUSTARD	Substitute fat-free half-and-half for evaporated milk. Use 3 whole eggs plus 2 egg whites. Bake 80–90 minutes.
COCONUT CUSTARD	Use only 1 teaspoon vanilla and add ½ teaspoon coconut extract. Sprinkle 1 teaspoon toasted coconut into each cup with milk mixture. Eliminate nutmeg and garnish each cup with 1 additional teaspoon toasted coconut *after* baking (adds 20 calories, 1.5 grams fat, 1 gram protein).
COFFEE CUSTARD	Add 1 tablespoon instant coffee powder to milk. Increase Splenda to ¾ cup. Eliminate nutmeg.
EGGNOG	Use only 1 teaspoon vanilla and add ½ teaspoon rum extract. Use 3 whole eggs and eliminate egg whites.

FLUFFY TAPIOCA PUDDING

A couple of simple changes are all it took to lighten up this old-fashioned favorite.

2½ cups 1% milk	1½ teaspoons vanilla
1 large egg, separated	¼ teaspoon cream of tartar
½ cup Splenda Granular	2 teaspoons sugar
3½ tablespoons quick-cooking tapioca	

1. In a medium saucepan combine milk, egg yolk, Splenda, and tapioca; let sit for 5 minutes to soften tapioca.
2. Whisk milk mixture thoroughly and place on stove. Bring to a boil while stirring. Remove from heat, stir in vanilla, and let set (it will thicken as it cools).
3. In a small bowl beat egg white and cream of tartar until foamy. Sprinkle in sugar and beat to soft peaks. Gently fold egg white into hot pudding. Let cool at least 20 minutes before serving or pouring into bowl or serving dishes. If not served warm, refrigerate.

Serves Six (½ cup)

PER SERVING

Calories 90	Fat 2 grams (1 saturated)
Carbohydrate 14 grams	Fiber 0 grams
Protein 4 grams	Sodium 100 milligrams

Diabetic exchange = ½ Low-fat Milk, ½ Carbohydrate
WW point comparison = 2 points

Tapioca does not respond well to "overdoing." Overcooking or overstirring tapioca (once it thickens) will create a gluey pudding.

CREAMY RICE PUDDING

I can't tell you how many pots of rice pudding I made (and ate!) to get this right.

1 cup cold water	⅛ teaspoon salt
½ cup medium-grain uncooked white rice	2 teaspoons cornstarch + 1 tablespoon water
3 cups 1% milk	1½ teaspoons vanilla
1 cup fat-free half and half	¼ teaspoon almond extract
½ cup Splenda Granular	½ teaspoon lemon zest
1 tablespoon butter	

1. In a medium saucepan bring water to a boil and stir in rice. Reduce to simmer, cover, and cook for 15–20 minutes or until water is absorbed.
2. Stir in milk, half-and-half, Splenda, butter, and salt. Cook, uncovered, over medium heat for 30 minutes, stirring frequently.
3. Add cornstarch mixture, heat until bubbling, and cook just until pudding thickens. Stir in vanilla, almond extract, and lemon zest. Pour into serving bowl or dessert dishes.

OLD-FASHIONED VARIATION: Eliminate lemon zest and top pudding with cinnamon.

Serves Eight (½ cup)

PER SERVING

Calories 130
Carbohydrate 21 grams
Protein 4 grams

Fat 2.5 grams (1.5 saturated)
Fiber 0.5 grams
Sodium 100 milligrams

Diabetic exchange = ½ Low-fat Milk, 1 Carbohydrate
WW point comparison = 3 points

For a lovely summer dessert, top each serving with ¼ cup fresh blueberries (adds 20 calories and 1 gram of fiber; does not change diabetic exchange or WW points.)

BAKED BROWN RICE PUDDING

Brown rice is higher in protein and fiber and has a lower glycemic index (the rate at which carbohydrates convert to sugar in the body) than white rice does. Brown rice also makes a nutritious and delicious rice pudding.

1¼ cups water	2 eggs, beaten
½ teaspoon cinnamon	1½ teaspoons vanilla
¼ teaspoon salt	1 teaspoon orange zest
½ cup brown rice	⅓ cup Splenda Granular
2½ cups 1% milk	½ teaspoon cinnamon

1. Preheat oven to 325°F.
2. In a medium saucepan bring water, ½ teaspoon cinnamon, and salt to a boil. Stir in rice. Cover and cook for 35-45 minutes or until most of the water is absorbed.
3. Stir milk, eggs, vanilla, orange zest, and Splenda into rice. Bring mixture to a simmer and transfer to a 2-quart casserole or baking dish.
4. Bake, uncovered, for 30 minutes; stir. Bake additional 30 minutes and stir again. Remove from oven and swirl in last ½ teaspoon cinnamon. Pudding will continue to thicken as it cools. Serve warm or chilled.

Serves Six (½ cup)

PER SERVING

Calories 135	Fat 2 grams (1 saturated)
Carbohydrate 18 grams	Fiber 1 gram
Protein 7 grams	Sodium 120 milligrams

Diabetic exchange = ½ Low-fat Milk, ½ Carbohydrate, ½ Lean Meat
WW point comparison = 2 points

Sliced almonds would make a nice garnish for this pudding.

NEW ORLEANS BREAD PUDDING WITH BOURBON SAUCE

Bread puddings are the quintessential comfort food. Maybe that's why in these stressful times there has been such a resurgence in their popularity. The Bourbon Sauce, a New Orleans tradition, complements the bread pudding beautifully both in taste and appearance.

5 cups slightly dried-out French or Italian bread, cubed (1–2-inch pieces)	2 large egg whites
1½ cups 1% milk	1½ teaspoons cinnamon
1 cup fat-free half-and-half	1 tablespoon vanilla
¾ cup Splenda Granular	2 teaspoons granulated sugar
2 large eggs	½ teaspoon cinnamon
	Bourbon Sauce (page 268)

1. Preheat oven to 350°F. Spray 8-inch square baking pan with non-stick cooking spray. Spread bread cubes in pan.
2. In medium bowl, whisk together next 7 ingredients (milk through vanilla). Pour over bread cubes. Let set about 10 minutes, pressing top cubes down to saturate.
3. Mix together granulated sugar and cinnamon. Sprinkle on top of pudding. Bake for one hour until center of pudding puffs.
4. Cool at least 15 minutes or entirely before serving. Serve warm (reheat briefly in microwave) or at room temperature with warmed Bourbon Sauce.

Serves Six (½ cup)

PER SERVING

Calories 185 (with 1½ tablespoons sauce)
Carbohydrate 24 grams
Protein 8 grams

Fat 4.5 grams (2 saturated)
Fiber 1 gram
Sodium 125 milligrams

Diabetic exchange = ½ Low-fat Milk, 1 Carbohydrate, 1 Fat
WW point comparison = 4 points

Bread pudding is thought to have originated in England in the late 1600s. If anyone has adopted it as their own here in the United States it's New Orleans, well known for its bread puddings.

STRAWBERRY FOOL

A fool is an old-fashioned English dessert made by swirling pureed fruit into whipped cream. This lighter version uses a small amount of real whipped cream but combines it with yogurt to lighten it up—as fat and calories are significantly reduced.

1½ cups low-fat plain yogurt

8 tablespoons Splenda Granular, divided

½ teaspoon almond extract (optional)

12 ounces fresh strawberries, washed and stemmed

4 tablespoons heavy whipping cream

1. In a small bowl, combine yogurt, 4 tablespoons Splenda, and extract if desired. In a separate bowl, mash berries with 2 tablespoons Splenda. Chill both at least one hour.
2. Whip cream with remaining 2 tablespoons Splenda until moderately stiff. Fold cream into yogurt mixture. Swirl strawberry mixture into yogurt/cream mixture. Serve.

Serves Four (¾ cup)

PER SERVING

Calories 140

Carbohydrate 16 grams

Protein 6 grams

Fat 6 grams (3 saturated)

Fiber 2 grams

Sodium 70 milligrams

Diabetic exchange = ½ Low-fat Milk, ½ Fruit, 1 Fat

WW point comparison = 3 points

"Fool" is from the French word *fouler*, meaning "to crush."

FRENCH CREAM WITH RASPBERRY SAUCE

French Cream is a creamy concoction comprised of sweetened heavy cream, sour cream, and cream cheese. This lightened version is elegant and delicious enough for the fanciest of celebrations and yet is easy enough to make anytime.

1	8-ounce tub light cream cheese	¼	teaspoon almond extract
1	cup fat-free sour cream	1	cup raspberries
1¼	cups fat-free half-and-half	2	tablespoons Splenda Granular
1	envelope unflavored gelatin	1	tablespoon orange liqueur or water
¾	cup Splenda Granular		
2	tablespoons vanilla		

1. Set aside six 4–6-ounce custard cups or ramekins. In a medium bowl, beat cream cheese and sour cream until smooth.
2. In a small saucepan, combine half-and-half and gelatin. Let set 3 minutes. Whisk in ¾ cup Splenda and place over medium heat. Cook, stirring, until gelatin dissolves (1–2 minutes). Pour gelatin mixture, vanilla, and almond extract into cream cheese mixture and beat until completely smooth.
3. Divide mixture evenly among the custard cups. Cover and refrigerate.
4. Pulse berries, 2 tablespoons Splenda, and liqueur in food processor or blender until smooth. Strain if desired. Unmold French Cream by dipping cups quickly in warm water and loosening edges with tip of knife. Place onto serving plate and drizzle with raspberry sauce.

Serves Six (½ cup)

PER SERVING

Calories 200	Fat 6 grams (4 saturated)
Carbohydrate 21 grams	Fiber 1 grams
Protein 8 grams	Sodium 210 milligrams

Diabetic exchange = 1 Low-fat Milk, ½ Carbohydrate
WW point comparison = 4 points

Classic French coeur a la crème ("hearts filled with cream") can contain up to 48 grams of fat per serving (with 30 of them saturated)!

ORANGE SNOW

This is truly a sweet nothing. Very low in calories, fat, and carbs, it is quite light and refreshing. The perfect treat for a hot summer's day.

1½ teaspoons unflavored gelatin	¼ cup orange juice
2 tablespoons cold water	1 tablespoon orange zest
1 egg yolk	2 egg whites
1 cup buttermilk	2 tablespoons Splenda Granular
½ cup Splenda Granular	

1. Place gelatin in a small bowl and add water. Set aside.
2. In a medium saucepan whisk together egg yolk, buttermilk, and ½ cup Splenda. Heat mixture until it thickens slightly (enough to coat a spoon). Stir in softened gelatin, orange juice, and zest. Remove from heat, pour into bowl, and cool mixture in refrigerator until it reaches the consistency of raw egg whites.
3. Whip egg whites until foamy. Add 2 tablespoons Splenda and beat to soft peaks. Fold into orange mixture. Refrigerate until ready to serve.

Serves Four (½ cup)

PER SERVING

Calories 65	Fat 2 grams (1 saturated)
Carbohydrate 8 grams	Fiber 0 grams
Protein 5 grams	Sodium 95 milligrams

Diabetic exchange = ½ Low-fat Milk
WW point comparison = 1 point

Buttermilk is a naturally low-fat food.

PUMPKIN MOUSSE WITH GINGERSNAPS

This creamy, spicy mousse is a perfect sweet and luscious dessert for heavy, rich holiday meals.

2 teaspoons unflavored gelatin	2 teaspoons cinnamon
¼ cup cold water	1½ teaspoons nutmeg
1 cup boiling water	½ teaspoon allspice
½ cup low-fat cottage cheese	1 cup light whipped topping
½ cup low-fat plain yogurt	6 gingersnap cookies (like Nabisco Old Fashioned), finely crushed
1 15-ounce can pumpkin (not pie filling)	
¾ cup Splenda Granular	2 tablespoons Splenda Granular

1. Sprinkle gelatin over ¼ cup of cold water in a small bowl. Let sit for 3 minutes. Add 1 cup boiling water and stir.
2. Puree cottage cheese and yogurt in a food processor or blender until completely smooth. Transfer to a large bowl. Add gelatin mixture, pumpkin, ¾ cup Splenda, and spices. Beat with electric mixer until smooth. Fold in whipped topping. Spoon mousse into individual serving dishes or a 1½–2-quart bowl or soufflé dish.
3. In a small bowl combine crushed gingersnaps and 2 tablespoons Splenda. Sprinkle over top of mousse. Refrigerate for at least 2 hours.

Serves Eight

PER SERVING

Calories 90	Fat 2 grams (1.5 saturated)
Carbohydrate 13 grams	Fiber 2 grams
Protein 4 grams	Sodium 90 milligrams

Diabetic exchange = 1 Vegetable, ½ Carbohydrate
WW point comparison = 2 points

Just one serving of this luscious dessert will give you 200 percent of your daily requirement of vitamin A.

DARK CHOCOLATE MOUSSE

This recipe is for the "reader from Philadelphia" who so kindly gave my first book a five-star review on Amazon.com and requested a creamy, dark, dense chocolate mousse. I hope this is what you were looking for!

1 teaspoon unflavored gelatin	⅓ cup unsweetened Dutch-processed cocoa powder
2 tablespoons water	2 ounces semisweet chocolate, chopped
¾ cup fat-free half-and-half	
1 teaspoon orange zest	1 teaspoon vanilla
2 eggs, separated	1 tablespoon sugar
⅔ cup Splenda Granular	¾ cup light whipped topping

1. In a small saucepan combine gelatin and water. Let set for 3 minutes. Add nonfat half-and-half and orange zest. Whisk in 2 egg yolks, Splenda, and cocoa powder. Place on medium heat and cook, stirring, until mixture is smooth and thickened (about 3–4 minutes).
2. Add chopped chocolate and vanilla and stir until smooth. Let cool to room temperature (about 30 minutes).
3. In a large bowl, beat egg whites until frothy. Beat in sugar until soft peaks form. Gently fold egg white into chocolate mixture. Fold in light whipped topping. Refrigerate until very cold.

Serves Six (½ cup)

PER SERVING

Calories 150
Carbohydrate 18 grams
Protein 4 grams

Fat 5.5 grams (3.5 saturated)
Fiber 2 grams
Sodium 25 milligrams

Diabetic exchange = 1 Non-fat Milk, ½ Carbohydrate, 1 Fat
WW point comparison = 3 points

Cocoa powder is naturally acidic. When treated with an alkali to reduce this acidity, it is called Dutch-processed. Dutch-processed cocoa has a darker color and is less bitter than natural cocoa.

Frozen Desserts

HISTORY DATES THE FIRST SWEET, FROZEN DESSERTS TO CHINA, WHERE they reportedly combined snow with milk or fruit syrups to make what would now be closer to sherbet than ice cream. Whether it is truth or myth that it was Marco Polo who took the recipes back to the Roman Empire is uncertain, but accounts of emperors indulging in frozen desserts can be found. As the new found frozen treats spread through Europe in the seventeenth century, sorbets and sherbets became prevalent foods on the tables of royalty. It took the development of custard to create what we now know as ice cream. In eighteenth-century New England, Thomas Jefferson and George Washington were reputed to be two of America's first ice-cream fans. It was here that the first portable hand-cranked ice-cream maker was invented, along with large-scale production, and sales took off.

Today, the varieties of frozen dessert products are endless. From the simple and ultrarich to no-fat, no-sugar concoctions with long lists of unpronounceable ingredients, there is something for everyone. There are many advantages, however, to making your own. First of all, making your own is fun! Not only is it fun, it is easier than ever. Compared to old-fashioned tubs, the new ice-cream machines with electric motors requiring no salt or ice are a snap to use (and to clean up). They also produce great low-sugar desserts in no time at all—freezing time is less than 30 minutes. Another advantage of making your own frozen dessert is that *you* can control all of the ingredients. To that end I have included a recipe for no-added-sugar Berry Sorbet and a wonderful Buttermilk Boysenberry Sherbet, two great treats I have yet to see in the market. Because sugar is necessary for these frozen desserts to remain scoopable when frozen, manufacturers simply don't make them. But you can. To bring them back to a softer consistency after freezing, simply place them in the refrigerator for at least 30 minutes. I also offer some great ice creams with my High Protein Vanilla Soft Serve and Lemon Cheesecake Ice Cream, which are higher in protein and lower in carbohydrate than even many of the no-sugar versions. Last, when making your own, you can create new flavor combinations—simply alter the recipes by changing the type of fruit you use or adding in your favorite flavorings.

FROZEN DESSERTS

Chocolate Sorbet
Berry Sorbet
Buttermilk Boysenberry Sherbet
Peach Frozen Yogurt
Strawberry Frozen Yogurt
High-Protein Vanilla Soft Serve
Creamy French Vanilla Frozen Custard
Vanilla Ice Cream in a Bag
Lemon Cheesecake Ice Cream
Café au Lait Ice Cream

CHOCOLATE SORBET

Just a little goes a long way with this intense, dark, chocolate sorbet. A mere tablespoon of corn syrup really helps to smooth both the texture and the flavor.

1 cup Splenda Granular	1 ½ cups water
⅔ cup Dutch-processed cocoa powder	1 tablespoon light corn syrup
	1 teaspoon vanilla

1. Combine Splenda and cocoa powder in medium saucepan. Whisk in water and corn syrup. Place over medium heat and bring to a boil. Reduce heat and simmer 4–5 minutes or until slightly thickened.
2. Remove from heat, pour into bowl, and stir in vanilla. Chill 30 minutes.
3. Pour sorbet into ice-cream maker and freeze according to manufacturer's directions. Serve immediately or place into container and freeze.
4. Before serving, place sorbet in refrigerator for 30 minutes to soften.

Serves Six (⅓ cup)

PER SERVING

Calories 60	Fat 1 gram (0.5 saturated)
Carbohydrate 10 grams	Fiber 3 grams
Protein 2 grams	Sodium 10 milligrams

Diabetic exchange = ½ Carbohydrate
WW point comparison = 1 point

Made with granulated sugar, a serving of this sorbet would contain 30 grams of carbohydrate.

BERRY SORBET

Bursting with the flavor of fresh berries, this beautiful ruby red sorbet is truly a delight to the taste buds.

1 **quart fresh strawberries or raspberries, stemmed, washed, and sliced**	1 **teaspoon orange zest**
2 **tablespoons orange juice**	⅔ **cup Splenda Granular**
	½ **cup water**

1. Puree berries with orange juice and zest in food processor or blender. Set aside.
2. In a small saucepan bring Splenda and water to a boil. Reduce heat and simmer for 5 minutes until slightly thickened. Add syrup to berries. Cool.
3. Pour sorbet into ice-cream maker and freeze according to manufacturer's directions. Serve immediately or place into container and freeze.
4. Before serving, place sorbet in refrigerator for 30 minutes to soften.

Serves Six (½ cup)

PER SERVING

Calories 35
Carbohydrate 8 grams
Protein 0 grams

Fat 0 grams (0 saturated)
Fiber 2 grams
Sodium 0 milligrams

Diabetic exchange = ½ Fruit
WW point comparison = 1 point

Marco Polo is credited for bringing the first recipes for fruit ices or sorbets to Europe from the Orient.

BUTTERMILK BOYSENBERRY SHERBET

The tartness of buttermilk combines beautifully with fresh or frozen boysenberries for a delicious sherbet low in sugar as well as fat.

1 teaspoon unflavored gelatin	⅔ cup Splenda Granular
1 teaspoon orange juice	⅔ cup water
1½ cups fresh or thawed frozen boysenberries	1 cup buttermilk

1. In a small bowl, sprinkle gelatin over orange juice. Set aside.
2. In a medium saucepan combine boysenberries, Splenda, and water. Place over medium heat and simmer for 5 minutes. Remove from heat and add gelatin. Stir to dissolve. Strain mixture through a sieve to remove seeds.
3. Combine berry syrup with buttermilk. Pour sherbet into ice-cream maker and freeze according to manufacturer's directions. Serve immediately or place into container and freeze.
4. Before serving, place sherbet in refrigerator for 30 minutes to soften.

Serves Four (½ cup)

PER SERVING

Calories 60	Fat 0.5 gram (0 saturated)
Carbohydrate 12 grams	Fiber 2 grams
Protein 3 grams	Sodium 55 milligrams

Diabetic exchange = ½ Fruit, ½ Non-fat Milk
WW point comparison = 1 point

Use a large spoon and press on berries to force pulp through the sieve or strainer.

PEACH FROZEN YOGURT

While nothing beats the taste of a fresh peach in season, you have the option of using frozen peaches in this recipe so you can enjoy the fresh taste of summer all year long.

2 cups peeled peach slices, fresh or frozen, thawed	¾ cup fat-free half-and-half
¾ cup Splenda Granular	¾ cup Splenda Granular
1½ teaspoons unflavored gelatin	1½ cups low-fat plain yogurt
	½ teaspoon vanilla

1. In a food processor, puree peaches and Splenda. Set aside.
2. Combine gelatin and ¼ cup half-and-half. Let set 3 minutes. Whisk in remaining half-and-half and Splenda. Heat just until gelatin dissolves. Cool slightly and stir in yogurt and vanilla.
3. Pour yogurt into ice-cream maker and freeze according to manufacturer's directions. Serve immediately or place into container and freeze.
4. Before serving, place yogurt in refrigerator for 30 minutes to soften.

Serves Eight (½ cup)

PER SERVING

Calories 100
Carbohydrate 16 grams
Protein 4 grams

Fat 1 gram (0.5 saturated)
Fiber 1 gram
Sodium 45 milligrams

Diabetic exchange = ½ Fruit, ½ Low-fat Milk
WW point comparison = 2 points

Peaches are customarily served at birthday celebrations in China as a symbol of hope and longevity.

STRAWBERRY FROZEN YOGURT

It doesn't get any easier than this.

1 quart fresh strawberries, stemmed, washed, and halved	**¾ cup Splenda Granular**
	1 cup low-fat plain yogurt
	¾ cup 1% milk
1 tablespoon lemon juice	

1. Place berries on a cookie sheet and partially freeze (15–30 minutes). Remove from freezer and coarsely puree berries with lemon juice.
2. In a large bowl combine Splenda, yogurt, low-fat milk, and berries.
3. Pour yogurt into ice-cream maker and freeze according to manufacturer's directions. Serve immediately or place into container and freeze.
4. Before serving, place yogurt in refrigerator for 30 minutes to soften.

Serves Six (½ cup)

PER SERVING

Calories 70
Carbohydrate 11 grams
Protein 3 grams

Fat 1 gram (0.5 saturated)
Fiber 2 grams
Sodium 45 milligrams

Diabetic exchange = ½ Non-fat Milk, ½ Fruit
WW point comparison = 1 point

HIGH-PROTEIN VANILLA SOFT SERVE

My boys really enjoy eating this easy-to-make, delicious soft-serve-style ice cream. Little do they know it is actually a good source of calcium. Drizzle the Dark Chocolate Sauce (page 269) on it for a real treat.

1 teaspoon unflavored gelatin	½ cup nonfat dry milk
1 tablespoon water	⅔ cup Splenda Granular
1 cup 1% milk	1½ cups whole milk
¼ cup egg substitute	1 teaspoon vanilla extract

1. In a medium saucepan sprinkle gelatin over water. Let set 3 minutes.
2. Add low-fat milk and place over low heat until gelatin dissolves. Remove from heat and add remaining ingredients.
3. Pour ice cream into ice-cream maker and freeze according to manufacturer's directions. Serve immediately or place into container and freeze.
4. Before serving, place ice cream in refrigerator for 30 minutes to soften.

Serves Six

PER SERVING

Calories 100
Carbohydrate 11 grams
Protein 7 grams

Fat 3.5 grams (2 saturated)
Fiber 0 grams
Sodium 100 milligrams

Diabetic exchange = 1 Low-fat Milk
WW point comparison = 2 points

CREAMY FRENCH VANILLA FROZEN CUSTARD

The pasteurized egg substitute works beautifully to create a "no-cook" creamy custard base for this simple yet delicious, rich-tasting frozen custard. The high egg ratio gives this "French" custard not only its name but its characteristic yellow color.

1 cup light cream	¾ cup egg substitute
1 cup 1% milk	(I prefer Egg Beaters)
1 cup Splenda Granular	2 teaspoons vanilla

1. In a large container whisk together light cream, milk, Splenda, egg substitute, and vanilla.
2. Pour custard into ice-cream maker and freeze according to manufacturer's directions. Serve immediately or place into container and store in freezer.
3. Before serving, place frozen custard in refrigerator for at least 30 minutes to soften.

Serves Six (½ cup)

PER SERVING

Calories 120
Carbohydrate 8 grams
Protein 5 grams

Fat 7 grams (4 saturated)
Fiber 0 grams
Sodium 85 milligrams

Diabetic exchange = ½ Milk, I Fat
WW point comparison = 2 points

To keep this recipe simple, I have used pure vanilla extract. If you scrape the inside of a vanilla bean into the custard in place of the extract, it will produce a lovely vanilla bean—flecked frozen custard.

VANILLA ICE CREAM IN A BAG

"Baggie Ice Cream" is an old stand-by for camp outs with the kids. A colleague of mine uses this version for her kids at diabetes camp each summer, but it will also work well in your own backyard or as something the kids can do on a rainy afternoon.

1 **gallon freezer bag, zip type**	½ **cup or 12 packets Splenda Granular**
Cubed or crushed ice	1 **teaspoon vanilla**
6 **tablespoons salt**	1 **quart freezer bag, zip type**
2 **cups fat-free half-and-half**	

1. Fill half the gallon-sized bag with cubed or crushed ice; add 6 tablespoons salt to the ice.
2. Mix the half-and-half, Splenda, and vanilla in the 1-quart freezer bag and zip closed. Place it inside the larger bag; zip closed. Squish and shake for about 5 minutes or until the ice cream thickens.

Serves Four (½ cup)

PER SERVING

Calories 90
Carbohydrate 15 grams
Protein 2 grams

Fat 0 grams (0 saturated)
Fiber 0 grams
Sodium 80 milligrams

Diabetic exchange = 1 Carbohydrate
WW point comparison = 2 points

LEMON CHEESECAKE ICE CREAM

This recipe is for me, because I love ice cream, I enjoy cheesecake, and lemon is one of my favorite flavors—and this recipe satisfies all three. The warmed milk mixture helps to cream the ricotta in order to give this ice cream a smoother texture than a traditional ricotta cheesecake. Enjoy!

½ cup light ricotta
¼ cup each light cream cheese and light sour cream
¼ cup lemon juice
Zest of one lemon

½ teaspoon vanilla
¼ teaspoon almond extract
1½ cups fat-free half-and-half
¾ cup Splenda Granular
2 eggs beaten

1. Place first 7 ingredients (ricotta to almond extract) in food processor or blender.
2. In a medium saucepan combine half-and-half, Splenda, and eggs. Place on medium heat and cook 4–5 minutes until mixture thickens and coats a spoon. Slowly pour mixture into ricotta mixture and blend until smooth. Chill 20–30 minutes.
3. Pour into ice-cream maker and freeze according to manufacturer's directions. Serve immediately or place into container and freeze.
4. Before serving, place ice cream in refrigerator for 30 minutes to soften.

Serves Six (½ cup)

PER SERVING

Calories 135
Carbohydrate 12 grams
Protein 7 grams

Fat 6 grams (2.5 saturated)
Fiber 0 grams
Sodium 110 milligrams

Diabetic exchange = 1 Low-fat Milk, 1 Fat
WW point comparison = 3 points

Café au Lait Ice Cream

You don't have to be a coffee drinker to enjoy the great taste of this cool treat.

- 2 eggs, beaten
- ¾ cup Splenda Granular
- 1½ cups 1% milk
- 2 teaspoons cornstarch
- 2 tablespoons instant coffee granules
- ¼ cup miniature marshmallows
- 1 cup fat-free half-and-half

1. In medium saucepan whisk together first 4 ingredients (eggs through cornstarch) and heat until mixture reaches a low boil. Add coffee granules. Stir in marshmallows. Set aside to cool for 15 minutes. Add half-and-half and cool.
2. Pour mixture into ice-cream maker and freeze according to manufacturer's directions. Serve immediately or place into container and freeze.
3. Before serving, place ice cream in refrigerator for 30 minutes to soften.

Serves Six (½ cup)

Per Serving

Calories 100
Carbohydrate 13 grams
Protein 5 grams

Fat 2.5 grams (1 saturated)
Fiber 3 grams
Sodium 60 milligrams

Diabetic exchange = ½ Low-fat Milk, ½ Carbohydrate
WW point comparison = 2 points

For an interesting flavor combination, dust ice cream with ground cinnamon just before serving.

Irresistible Cookies

B Y BAKING STANDARDS, COOKIES ARE QUITE SIMPLE TO MAKE—OFTEN only a few easy steps are required—and the results are almost immediate (especially if you count nibbling on the dough). However, when it comes to taking out the sugar, things can get a bit complicated, which is why just using a sugar substitute in a recipe can have "interesting and sometimes inedible" results. Here's why.

According to well-respected food scientist and cookbook author Shirley O. Corriher, cookies are a "microcosm of baking," in which each ingredient has a huge effect on the finished cookie. The major ingredient groups for most cookies are flour, sugar (or sweeteners), fat, leaveners (like baking powder and baking soda), eggs, and occasionally liquids. Sugar is a critical component, as it affects not only the sweetness, but the color, the texture, and the amount of spread (or height) of the cookie. The type and amount of fat used also affects color and spread. That is why when the sugar is reduced in a cookie recipe, the fat is increased and vice versa. Reducing both the sugar and the fat in a cookie recipe is a challenge. But I am happy to tell you that it's possible and the following recipes prove it. What I found is that including just a tablespoon or two of the "right" type of sugar in a recipe makes all the difference. Doing this has allowed me to offer you terrific, great-tasting, low-sugar versions of some favorite types of cookies. You'll have your choice of bar cookies to make like Creamy Lemon Bars and chocolate Zebra Bars, which are renditions of classic favorites, and a High Protein Peanut Butter Oat Bar that meets today's need for higher protein and less sugar.

You'll also find recipes for drop cookies, like Coconut Crispy Macaroons, and versatile soft Sour Cream Sugar Cookies. And last, but certainly not least, if you love to work with cookie dough, you will have great fun in shaping up two wonderful versions of crunchy biscotti and the kid-pleasing Molasses Cutouts. Let's bake cookies!

IRRESISTIBLE COOKIES

Creamy Lemon Bars

Zebra Bars

High-Protein Peanut Butter Oat Bars

Italian Meringue Cookies

Orange Oatmeal Cookies

Coconut Crispy Macaroons

Soft Sour Cream Sugar Cookies

Chocolate Almond Biscotti

Orange Ginger Pecan Biscotti

Molasses Cutouts

CREAMY LEMON BARS

Just like the traditional favorite: creamy, sweet, and tart lemon topping on top of a buttery crust. Be sure to use fresh lemon juice and zest for best results.

CRUST

1	cup all-purpose flour
⅓	cup Splenda Granular
½	teaspoon lemon zest
4	tablespoons margarine or butter
2	tablespoons light cream cheese

TOPPING

2	large eggs + 2 egg whites

6	tablespoons lemon juice
1	cup Splenda Granular
1½	tablespoons light corn syrup
1	tablespoon all-purpose flour
1½	teaspoons zest
½	teaspoon baking powder
2	teaspoons powdered sugar (optional)

1. Preheat oven to 375°F. Spray an 8-inch square pan with nonstick baking spray.

2. In a medium bowl mix together flour, Splenda, and lemon zest. Cut in margarine or butter. Mix in cream cheese until you have fine crumbs. Press onto the bottom of the prepared pan. Bake for 15 minutes.

3. While crust is baking, prepare topping. In a large bowl beat the eggs and egg whites with the lemon juice, Splenda, and corn syrup until frothy. Briefly beat in flour, zest, and baking powder. Pour over hot baked crust.

4. Turn down to 350°F and bake bars additional 18–20 minutes or until top is set. Cool completely.

5. Just prior to serving, dust with powdered sugar if desired.

Serves Twelve (1 bar)

PER SERVING

Calories 110
Carbohydrate 14 grams
Protein 3 grams

Fat 4.5 grams (2 saturated)
Fiber 1 gram
Sodium 80 milligrams

Diabetic exchange = 1 Carbohydrate, 1 Fat
WW point comparison = 2 points

ZEBRA BARS

Moist, dark chocolate bars swirled with sweetened cream cheese. These are hard to resist.

1	ounce semisweet chocolate	¾	cup all-purpose flour
2	tablespoons margarine	½	teaspoon baking powder
¼	cup prune puree or	¼	teaspoon baking soda
	1 2.5-ounce jar baby food prunes	½	cup cream cheese, light tub-style
3	tablespoons brown sugar	2	tablespoons egg white (reserved)
⅔	cup Splenda Granular		
¼	cup cocoa powder	2	tablespoons Splenda Granular
1	large egg + 2 egg whites		
1½	teaspoons vanilla	1	tablespoon powdered sugar
1	tablespoon hot tap water	½	teaspoon vanilla

1. Preheat oven to 325°F. Spray a 7 × 11- or 9 × 9-inch baking pan with nonstick cooking spray.
2. Melt chocolate and margarine together in medium bowl by microwaving on high for 30–60 seconds. Whisk in next 8 ingredients (reserving 2 tablespoons of egg white). Blend until smooth.
3. Sift in flour, baking powder, and baking soda. Mix just until flour is incorporated and pour batter into prepared baking pan.
4. In a small bowl beat together last 5 ingredients. Drop by teaspoonfuls onto top of chocolate batter. Pull knife through batter to create swirl pattern. Bake 20–22 minutes; just until center feels firm to touch.

Serves Fifteen (1 bar)

PER SERVING

Calories 90
Carbohydrate 12 grams
Protein 3 grams

Fat 4 grams (2 saturated)
Fiber 1 gram
Sodium 105 milligrams

Diabetic exchange = 1 Carbohydrate, ½ Fat
WW point comparison = 2 points

HIGH-PROTEIN PEANUT BUTTER OAT BARS

I sent a pan of these to school with my third-grade son. He brought back the empty pan and a stack of thank-you notes. Not too bad for a "healthy" cookie.

6 tablespoons chunky peanut butter	2 cups old-fashioned oats
3 tablespoons margarine, softened	½ cup nonfat milk powder
2 tablespoons honey	½ cup all-purpose flour
¾ cup Splenda Granular	¼ teaspoon salt
2 eggs	½ teaspoon baking powder
1½ teaspoons vanilla	¼ teaspoon baking soda
	1 ounce semisweet chocolate

1. Preheat oven to 350°F. Spray a 9 × 13-inch pan with nonstick cooking spray.
2. In large bowl beat together peanut butter, margarine, and honey. Add Splenda, eggs, and vanilla. Beat until fluffy (2–3 minutes). Stir in remaining ingredients except chocolate.
3. Press mixture into baking pan and bake for 12-14 minutes. Remove from oven.
4. In a small bowl, melt chocolate in microwave for 30–60 seconds. Stir and drizzle with a fork across bars. Cool, cut, and serve bars.

Serves Twenty (1 bar)

PER SERVING

Calories 95
Carbohydrate 10 grams
Protein 5 grams

Fat 5 grams (1 saturated)
Fiber 1 grams
Sodium 110 milligrams

Diabetic exchange = ½ Carbohydrate, 1 Medium-fat Meat
WW point comparison = 2 points

In the United States, 50 percent of all peanuts produced are turned into peanut butter, the very American staple.

ITALIAN MERINGUE COOKIES

There are two standard methods for making meringue cookies. There is the "common method" and the "Italian method." The "common" method of beating egg whites and sugar until stiff does not work using Splenda. But, the "Italian" method, where boiling sugar syrup is beaten into stiffened egg whites, does. Here Splenda can be substituted for most of the sugar in the recipe with great success.

¾   cup Splenda Granular
3   tablespoons sugar
⅔   cup water
3   egg whites
¼   teaspoon cream of tartar

½   teaspoon vanilla
½   teaspoon orange, lemon, peppermint, or other flavored extracts (optional)

1. Preheat oven to 275°F. Line baking sheet with parchment paper (or foil).
2. Combine Splenda, sugar, and water in a saucepan over moderately high heat. Swirl pan by its handle, but do not stir while syrup comes to a boil. Cover pan, reduce heat, and let simmer.
3. In a large bowl beat egg whites until foamy. Beat in cream of tartar and increase speed until egg whites form stiff peaks.
4. Remove cover from sugar syrup and insert candy thermometer. Boil syrup until it reaches 235°F. Immediately remove from stove and gradually add boiling syrup into egg whites while beating vigorously.
5. Beat in vanilla and any optional flavorings until mixture is very stiff (5–6 minutes).
6. Drop by tablespoonfuls or pipe through a pastry bag onto baking sheets. Bake 1 hour, turn off oven, and allow meringues to cool in oven until they can be easily removed from parchment paper.

Serves Nine (Two 2-inch cookies)

PER SERVING

Calories 30
Carbohydrate 6 grams
Protein 2 grams

Fat 0 grams (0 saturated)
Fiber 0 grams
Sodium 20 milligrams

Diabetic exchange = ½ Carbohydrate
WW point comparison = 1 point (up to 5 cookies for 1 point!)

According to Julia Child, perfectly baked meringues will not change shape or change color. The meringue mixture should simply dry out.

ORANGE OATMEAL COOKIES

I love the wonderful combination of orange and pecans in these delicate cookies. These are incredibly simple to make and even easier to eat.

3 tablespoons margarine or butter	**2 egg whites**
2 tablespoons corn syrup	**¾ cup old-fashioned oats**
1 tablespoon 1% milk	**¼ cup finely chopped pecans**
½ cup Splenda Granular	**2 tablespoons all-purpose flour**
1 teaspoon vanilla	**½ teaspoon baking soda**
	1 teaspoon orange zest

1. Preheat oven to 375°F. Lightly spray cookie sheet with nonstick baking spray.
2. In a medium saucepan melt margarine. Stir in corn syrup, milk, Splenda, and vanilla. Remove from heat and whisk in egg whites.
3. In a medium bowl mix together remaining ingredients. Pour margarine or butter mixture over dry ingredients and combine.
4. Drop wet batter by tablespoonful onto cookie sheets, flattening slightly. Bake 12–14 minutes. Cool slightly before removing.

Serves Sixteen (1 cookie)

PER SERVING

Calories 60
Carbohydrate 6 grams
Protein 1 gram

Fat 3.5 grams (0.5 saturated)
Fiber 1 gram
Sodium 70 milligrams

Diabetic exchange = ½ Low-fat Milk, ½ Carbohydrate
WW point comparison = 1 point

To produce flatter, crispier cookies, check cookies halfway through baking to see if they have puffed up. As soon as they do, firmly tap pan against oven rack, forcing them to flatten.

COCONUT CRISPY MACAROONS

These confection-like cookies use crispy rice cereal in place of some of the coconut in a traditional macaroon. The result is a terrific combination of crispy and chewy.

2	egg whites	1	teaspoon vanilla
	Pinch of cream of tartar	2	cups crispy rice cereal
3/4	cup Splenda Granular	1	cup unsweetened coconut

1. Preheat oven to 275°F. Spray baking sheets with non-stick cooking spray.*
2. In a large bowl beat egg whites and cream of tartar until soft peaks form. Gradually add Splenda and beat until stiff.
3. Fold in vanilla, cereal, and coconut. Drop by tablespoonfuls onto pans. Bake 18-20 minutes or until lightly browned and firm to touch.

Serves Twelve (2 cookies)

PER SERVING

Calories 70
Carbohydrate 7 grams
Protein 5 grams

Fat 4 grams (4 saturated)
Fiber 1 gram
Sodium 45 milligrams

Diabetic exchange = ½ Low-fat Milk, ½ Carbohydrate
WW point comparison = 1 point

*Lining baking sheets with parchment or using silicone baking mats (like Silplat) work especially well with macaroons.

SOFT SOUR CREAM SUGAR COOKIES

To be able to make soft, tender "sugar" cookies with so little sugar is amazing. This recipe can also be used as a base recipe for any sugar cookie variation. You may choose one of your own, or use one of the two I've provided. I particularly enjoy the citrus flavor. To make this recipe as a rolled cookie, add one additional tablespoon flour and chill dough before rolling out (⅛-inch thick) and cutting into desired shapes.

1½ cups all-purpose flour	2 tablespoons corn syrup
½ teaspoon baking soda	¼ cup sour cream
½ teaspoon baking powder	1 teaspoon vanilla
⅓ cup margarine	¼ teaspoon almond extract
¾ cup Splenda Granular	1 egg yolk

1. Preheat oven to 375°F. Lightly spray baking sheet with nonstick cooking spray.
2. In a small bowl sift together flour, baking soda, and baking powder. Set aside.
3. In a medium bowl with an electric mixer, beat together margarine, Splenda, and corn syrup until creamy. Add sour cream, vanilla, almond extract, and egg yolk. Beat 2–3 minutes until light and fluffy.
4. Stir in flour mixture.
5. Drop by tablespoonful onto baking sheet. Press down on dough with bottom of glass or spatula to flatten. Bake 3 minutes; tap pan against baking rack to flatten cookies; bake 4–5 more minutes.

CITRUS VARIATION: Add one teaspoon lemon, lime, or orange zest to batter.
SNICKERDOODLE VARIATION: Mix together one tablespoon each Splenda and granulated sugar with 2 teaspoons cinnamon. Roll 1 tablespoon dough in cinnamon/sugar mixture for each cookie. Flatten cookies with bottom of glass before baking.

Serves Twenty (1 cookie)

PER SERVING

Calories 70	Fat 3 grams (1 saturated)
Carbohydrate 10 grams	Fiber 0 grams
Protein 1 gram	Sodium 70 milligrams

Diabetic exchange = ½ Fat, ½ Carbohydrate
WW point comparison = 2 points

CHOCOLATE ALMOND BISCOTTI

In Italian, biscotti *means "twice baked." Baking them twice makes them crunchy and perfect for dipping. Serve biscotti with a cup of regular coffee or tea or choose one of the wonderful flavored versions from the "Delicious Drinks" chapter.*

¼ cup whole almonds	2 tablespoons butter
1¾ cups all-purpose flour	3 tablespoons brown sugar
¼ cup cocoa powder	¾ cup Splenda Granular
1 teaspoon baking powder	2 eggs + 1 egg white
¼ teaspoon baking soda	1 teaspoon almond extract
⅛ teaspoon salt	1 teaspoon vanilla extract

1. Preheat oven to 350°F. Lightly spray baking sheet with nonstick cooking spray.
2. Spread the almonds in a baking pan and place in oven. Bake for 5 minutes or until slightly browned. Remove and coarsely chop. Set aside.
3. In a medium bowl sift together flour, cocoa powder, baking powder, baking soda, and salt. Stir in almonds.
4. In a medium bowl cream butter and brown sugar with an electric mixer. Add Splenda, eggs, egg white, and almond and vanilla extracts. Beat until smooth. Fold in flour mixture with a spoon or spatula. Use hands to form dough into 2 "logs"—each 8 inches long and 2 inches wide. Place logs onto greased cookie sheet and flatten top slightly.
5. Bake for 30 minutes or until a toothpick inserted into the center comes out clean. Remove from oven and let cool 5–10 minutes. Reduce oven to 300°F. Slice ¼-inch slices on diagonal down log. Place cookies back on baking sheet and bake for 20 minutes longer until firm. Cookies will become firmer as they cool.

Serves Eighteen (2 cookies)

PER SERVING

Calories 90
Carbohydrate 12 grams
Protein 1 gram

Fat 3 grams (0 saturated)
Fiber 1 gram
Sodium 70 milligrams

Diabetic exchange = 1 Carbohydrate
WW point comparison = 2 points

Dough may crack along bottom edge of the biscotti due to expansion without sugar, which gives these biscotti a unique mushroom shape when sliced.

ORANGE GINGER PECAN BISCOTTI

Baking these fragrant cookies has become an annual holiday tradition for me. I love the compliments when I send them to friends and family. Package these with the Homemade Spiced Chai Mix (page 59) for a lovely hostess gift.

¼ cup pecan halves	2 whole eggs + I egg white
2 cups all-purpose flour	I tablespoon oil
¾ teaspoon ground ginger	2 tablespoons orange juice concentrate
½ teaspoon ground nutmeg	
I teaspoon baking powder	¾ cup Splenda Granular
¼ teaspoon baking soda	I tablespoon orange zest
I ½ tablespoons finely chopped crystallized ginger	

1. Preheat oven to 350°F. Lightly spray baking sheet with nonstick cooking spray.
2. Spread the pecans in a baking pan and place in oven. Bake for 5 minutes or until slightly browned. Remove and finely chop. Set aside.
3. In a medium bowl sift together flour, ginger, nutmeg, baking powder, baking soda, and ginger. Stir in pecans.
4. In a medium bowl whisk together remaining ingredients. Beat until smooth. Fold in flour mixture with a spoon or spatula. Use hands to form dough into 2 "logs"—each 8 inches long and 2 inches wide. Place logs onto greased cookie sheet and flatten top slightly.
5. Bake for 30 minutes or until a toothpick inserted into the center comes out clean. Remove from oven and let cool 5–10 minutes. Reduce oven to 300°F. Slice ¼-inch slices on diagonal down log. Place cookies back on baking sheet and bake for 20 minutes longer until firm. (Cookies will become firmer as they cool.)

Serves Thirty (1 cookie)

PER SERVING

Calories 50

Carbohydrate 9 grams

Protein 2 grams

Fat 1.5 grams (1 saturated)

Fiber 0 grams

Sodium 35 milligrams

Diabetic exchange = ½ Carbohydrate

WW point comparison = 1 point

 The traditional dunking cookie, known as biscotti, was enjoyed in Italy as early as the fourteenth century.

MOLASSES CUTOUTS

These cookies are a hit with kids! Not only do they love making and rolling out the dough, but they gobble them up and ask for more. This recipe is great for holiday cutouts like gingerbread men or as an accent to ice cream by cutting them out with a 2½-inch decorative biscuit cutter.

2	cups all-purpose flour	¼	cup prune puree or 1 jar baby food prunes (2.5-ounce)
2	teaspoons baking soda		
1	teaspoon cinnamon	¼	cup shortening
¾	teaspoon ginger	1	cup Splenda Granular
½	teaspoon cloves	3	tablespoons molasses
		1	large egg

1. Preheat oven to 350°F. Lightly spray baking sheet with nonstick cooking spray.
2. In a small bowl sift together flour, baking soda, cinnamon, ginger, and cloves. Set aside.
3. In a medium bowl with an electric mixer, beat together prunes, shortening, Splenda, molasses, and egg until creamy. Beat 2–3 minutes until light and fluffy.
4. Stir in flour mixture.
5. Divide the dough in half and wrap in plastic. Refrigerate until firm, at least 1 hour. (The dough can be refrigerated for up to 2 days.)
6. Remove 1 disk of dough from the refrigerator and cut in half. Return the unused portion to the refrigerator. Lightly flour a work surface. Roll the dough to ⅛-inch thickness and cut dough into desired shapes. Place on baking sheet. Bake 6–8 minutes.

GINGER COOKIE VARIATION: Simply roll one tablespoon dough for each cookie into a ball and place on baking sheet. Flatten with bottom of glass. Dust lightly with granulated sugar if desired prior to baking.

Serves Twenty-four (1 cookie)

PER SERVING

Calories 70
Carbohydrate 11 grams
Protein 1 gram

Fat 2.5 grams (1 saturated)
Fiber 1 gram
Sodium 135 milligrams

Diabetic exchange = 1 Carbohydrate
WW point comparison = 1 point

Classic Pies and More

I F YOU WANT TO IMPRESS SOMEONE, MAKE A CHEESECAKE. BUT IF YOU WANT someone to really feel welcomed or loved, make a pie! Pies are almost as old as time itself, dating back all the way to ancient Egypt. Originally, pies were made predominately of meat or seafood, but by the time the English settlers brought their traditions to America, fruit and custard had found their way into pies. Here in the land of plenty, especially in Pennsylvania Dutch country, homemakers quickly adopted pies as a new American tradition. Thus, pies as we know them today were born. These age-old classic pies have always represented the best of home-style cooking. Unfortunately, in today's harried world, not many cooks feel they have the time to make home-baked pies. Yet, that is why, more than ever, a home-baked pie is so welcomed.

What's not welcomed is the sugar, fat, and calories that many classic pies are filled with. Traditional pies can easily contain 500 calories, 60–75 grams of carbohydrate, and upwardsof 50 grams of fat per piece! (In fact, I recently came across a recipe for banana cream pie that contained 852 calories, 102 grams of carbohydrate, and 45 grams of fat—all packed into a single serving!)

In this chapter you will find some of my favorite versions of these classic pies, like rich and creamy Banana Cream in a graham-cracker crumb crust, plump and tender Sour Cream Apple with crumb topping, and deep, dark Chocolate Chiffon piled into a chocolate crust. I have also included a couple of newer American pies that are destined to become classics: sweet and tangy Key Lime and luscious Strawberry Dream. What's terrific about all of these pies (in addition to being reduced in calories, carbs, and fat) is that they are easy to make. In fact, not one requires you to roll out a hand-made crust, eliminating one of the most timely, and messy, aspects of traditional pies. To round out the pies, I offer "more"—a couple of delicious crisps, especially terrific when served up warm, and two fantastic phyllo creations—all certain to make anyone feel most welcomed or loved.

CLASSIC PIES AND MORE

Key Lime Pie

Banana Cream Pie

Sour Cream Apple Pie

Strawberry Dream Pie

Chocolate Chiffon Pie

Kim's Mixed Berry Crisp

Peach Blueberry Crisp with Almond Topping

Sweet Cheese Strudel

Phyllo Apple Packets

KEY LIME PIE

The highly aromatic Key Lime is the key to this famous Florida pie. These limes can be found in many markets during the summer months. If you can't find fresh limes, bottled key lime juice works in these recipes, too.

CRUST
1 cup graham-cracker crumbs
2 tablespoons Splenda Granular
1 tablespoon margarine or butter, melted
1 egg white

FILLING
1 envelope unflavored gelatin

⅔ cup key lime juice, divided
1 cup 1% milk
1 large egg + 2 egg yolks, lightly beaten
1 tablespoon lime zest
¾ cup Splenda Granular
4 ounces nonfat cream cheese
4 ounces light tub-style cream cheese

1. Preheat oven to 350°F. Lightly coat a 9-inch pie pan with nonstick cooking spray.
2. In a small bowl or food processor combine crumbs, Splenda, and margarine and pulse or stir. Add egg white and stir well, or pulse again. Pour crumb mixture into pie plate. With your fingers, the back of a spoon, or with a sheet of plastic wrap, press down on the crumbs until they coat the bottom and sides of the pie plate. Bake 8–10 minutes. Remove and cool.
3. In a medium saucepan dissolve the gelatin in ⅓ cup of the key lime juice for three minutes. Add milk, egg, egg yolks, remaining ⅓ cup key lime juice, lime zest, and Splenda. Cook for 10 minutes or until mixture thickens. Remove from heat. Cool slightly.
4. Place the cream cheeses in a large bowl and beat on medium speed with an electric mixer until creamy. Beat in lime mixture until smooth. Refrigerate mixture until thoroughly cooled, stirring every 10 minutes.
5. Pour mixture into cooled pie shell and chill at least 2 hours or overnight. Serve cool.

KEY LIME MOUSSE CUPS VARIATION: Beat 2 large pasteurized egg whites (or

1 nonpasteurized) and fold into cooked cooled custard. Pour Key Lime filling into 6 custard cups. (130 calories, 6 grams fat, 9 grams each carbohydrate and protein.)

Serves Eight

PER SERVING

Calories 160

Fat 6 grams (2.5 saturated)

Carbohydrate 16 grams

Fiber 0.5 gram

Protein 8 grams

Sodium 260 milligrams

Diabetic exchange = 1 Carbohydrate, 1 Fat

WW point comparison = 3 points

 Key lime pie is the official pie of Florida.

BANANA CREAM PIE

I didn't always get immediate feedback from my tasters when I left samples at their homes for them to try. I did with this one! They all loved it and called to let me know right away. (Maybe they were hoping for more?) The brandy extract is optional but truly adds great flavor to the filling.

VANILLA WAFER CRUST

1 generous cup crushed vanilla wafers (about 28 wafers)

1 tablespoon Splenda Granular

2 teaspoons margarine or butter, melted

1 tablespoon egg white

CREAM FILLING

1½ teaspoons unflavored gelatin

¼ cup 1% milk

1½ cups 1% milk

¾ cup nonfat half-and-half

¾ cup Splenda Granular

2 tablespoons cornstarch

1 egg + 1 egg white, lightly beaten

2 teaspoons vanilla

1 teaspoon brandy extract

1 large banana, thinly sliced

1 cup light whipped topping

1. Preheat oven to 350°F. Lightly coat a 9-inch pie pan with nonstick cooking spray.

2. Combine crumbs in a small bowl or food processor (pulse to make crumbs from wafers). Add Splenda and margarine, and stir or pulse. Add egg white and stir well, or pulse again. Pour crumb mixture into pie plate. With your fingers, the back of a spoon, or with a sheet of plastic wrap, press down on the crumbs until they coat the bottom and sides of the pie plate. Bake 8–10 minutes.

3. In a small saucepan sprinkle the gelatin over ¼ cup milk; let stand 3 minutes until softened. Set aside.

4. In a medium saucepan whisk together 1½ cups milk, half-and-half, Splenda, cornstarch, egg, and egg white until smooth. Cook over medium heat, stirring constantly, being sure to include edges of pot util pudding comes to a low boil. Then cook 1 minute more. Remove from the heat and stir in the dissolved gelatin, vanilla, and brandy extract. Set aside.

5. Spread ⅓ of the cream filling into the cooled pie shell. Top evenly with the sliced bananas, then spread the remaining cream filling evenly on top. Let cool to room temperature, then refrigerate until firm, about 2 hours.

6. Serve each slice with 2 tablespoons whipped topping, or, for a pretty touch, pipe the whipped topping all along the sides of the pie using a piping bag fitted with a large star tip.

Serves Eight

PER SERVING

Calories 180
Carbohydrate 24 grams
Protein 5 grams

Fat 7 grams (2.5 saturated)
Fiber 1 gram
Sodium 135 milligrams

Diabetic exchange = ½ Low-fat Milk, 1 Carbohydrate, 1 Fat
WW point comparison = 4 points

SOUR CREAM APPLE PIE

My goal was to create a truly old-fashioned, home-style recipe for apple pie and this recipe hit the mark. This pie has a creamy texture, a cinnamon flavor, and a wonderful aroma is sure to make any guest feel right at home. Prebaking the crust prevents the custard from making the crust soggy.

1 unbaked 9-inch pie crust	2½ cups peeled, thinly sliced, baking apples
2 large eggs	
1 cup light sour cream	**STREUSEL TOPPING**
¾ cup Splenda Granular	4 tablespoons all-purpose flour
2 tablespoons all-purpose flour	
2 teaspoons vanilla	3 tablespoons butter
¼ teaspoon salt	⅓ cup Splenda Granular
	1 teaspoon cinnamon

1. Preheat oven to 425°F. Bake pie crust for 15 minutes. Remove from oven. Cool. Set aside.
2. In a large bowl, lightly beat together eggs, sour cream, Splenda Granular, flour, vanilla, and salt. Stir in apples and pour into the prebaked pie shell. Bake for 15 minutes. Reduce heat to 350°F and bake for 20 minutes more, covering edges of piecrust with foil as needed to prevent overbrowning.
3. While pie is baking, combine the topping ingredients. Remove pie from oven and sprinkle on topping. Return pie to oven and bake an additional 20 minutes. Cool completely before serving.

Serves Eight

PER SERVING

Calories 190	Fat 11 grams (5 saturated)
Carbohydrate 20 grams	Fiber 1 gram
Protein 4 grams	Sodium 150 milligrams

Diabetic exchange = 1 Fruit, ½ Carbohydrate, 2 Fat
WW point comparison = 4 points

STRAWBERRY DREAM PIE

If you love your berries dished up with whipped cream, you'll love this pie.

VANILLA WAFER CRUST

1 generous cup crushed vanilla wafers (about 28 wafers)

1 tablespoon Splenda Granular

2 teaspoons margarine or butter, melted

1 tablespoon egg white

FILLING

2 cups sliced strawberries

2/3 cup Splenda Granular

1 tablespoon lemon juice

1 envelope unflavored gelatin

1/4 cup light cranberry juice

1 1/2 cups light whipped topping

1. Preheat oven to 350°F. Lightly coat a 9-inch pie pan with nonstick cooking spray.
2. Combine crumbs in a small bowl or food processor (pulse to make crumbs from wafers). Add Splenda and margarine, and stir or pulse. Add egg white and stir well, or pulse again. Pour crumb mixture into pie plate. With your fingers, the back of a spoon, or with a sheet of plastic wrap, press down on the crumbs until they coat the bottom and sides of the pie plate. Bake 8–10 minutes.
3. Mash the strawberries in a small bowl and stir in Splenda and lemon juice. Set aside for about 15 minutes, until the sugar dissolves and the mixture is very juicy.
4. Pour cranberry juice over gelatin. Let set 3 minutes. Heat to dissolve gelatin and cool slightly. Stir gelatin into strawberry mixture. Fold in light whipped topping. Pour into the pie shell and chill until firm, for at least 1 hour. Garnish with additional whip cream and a ring of whole strawberries.

Serves Seven

PER SERVING

Calories 170

Carbohydrate 21 grams

Protein 2 grams

Fat 9 grams (2 saturated)

Fiber 2 grams

Sodium 90 milligrams

Diabetic exchange = 1 Fruit, ½ Carbohydrate, 2 Fat

WW point comparison = 4 points

 A few simple changes was all it took to slash the carbohydrates in half and the fat by two-thirds!

CHOCOLATE CHIFFON PIE

Deep, dark chocolate filling in a deep, dark chocolate crust. Need I say more?

CHOCOLATE CRUST

- 1 cup chocolate graham-cracker crumbs (about 14 squares)
- 1 tablespoon Dutch-process cocoa powder (like Hershey's European)
- ¼ cup Splenda Granular
- 1 tablespoon margarine or butter, melted
- 1 large egg white

CHOCOLATE FILLING

- 1 envelope unflavored gelatin
- ¼ cup cold water
- ½ cup water
- 6 tablespoons cocoa powder
- 1 teaspoon cornstarch
- ½ cup Splenda Granular
- 3 egg yolks, lightly beaten
- 1 teaspoon vanilla
- 3 egg whites
- 2 tablespoons granulated sugar
- ¾ cup light whipped topping

1. Preheat oven to 350°F. Lightly coat a 9-inch pie pan with nonstick cooking spray.
2. Combine crumbs in a small bowl or food processor (pulse to make crumbs from crackers). Add cocoa powder, Splenda, and margarine, and stir or pulse. Add egg white and stir well, or pulse again. Pour crumb mixture into pie plate. With your fingers, the back of a spoon, or with a sheet of plastic wrap, press down on the crumbs until they coat the bottom and sides of the pie plate. Bake 8–10 minutes.
3. Soften gelatin in ¼ cup cold water. Set aside. Put ½ cup water in small saucepan. Whisk in cocoa, cornstarch, Splenda, and egg yolks. Place over medium heat and cook until thickened and smooth. Add softened gelatin and vanilla. Pour into a large bowl and let cool, stirring occasionally, until mixture mounds when dropped by spoon.
4. In a medium bowl beat egg whites until frothy. Add sugar and beat until stiff but not dry. Fold into chocolate mixture. Fold in whipped topping and pour into prepared crust.

MOCHA VARIATION: Use ½ cup strong coffee in place of ½ cup water.

Serves Eight

PER SERVING

Calories 160

Fat 6 grams (2 saturated)

Carbohydrate 21 grams

Fiber 2 grams

Protein 6 grams

Sodium 125 milligrams

Diabetic exchange = 1 Carbohydrate, 1 Fat
WW point comparison = 3 points

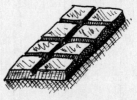

KIM'S MIXED BERRY CRISP

Kim, a lifetime member of Weight Watchers, not only sent me a thank-you for writing my dessert cookbook, she also sent me her favorite recipe, which I love and would like to share with you. Thanks, Kim.

2 16-ounce bags frozen mixed berries, thawed slightly
¾ cup Splenda Granular
1½ tablespoons cornstarch

TOPPING
¾ cup old-fashioned rolled oats
¾ cup Splenda Granular
¾ teaspoon cinnamon
1 tablespoon margarine
1 egg white

1. Preheat oven to 350°F. Set aside 9 × 13-inch pan.
2. In a large bowl toss berries with Splenda and cornstarch. Pour into pan.
3. In a small bowl cut margarine into oats, Splenda, and cinnamon. Gently stir in egg white and sprinkle over berries. Bake for 30 minutes or until bubbling.

Serves Eight

PER SERVING

Calories 135
Carbohydrate 28 grams
Protein 2 grams

Fat 2.5 grams (0 saturated)
Fiber 6 grams
Sodium 15 milligrams

Diabetic exchange = 1 Fruit, ½ Carbohydrate, ½ Fat
WW point comparison = 2 points

PEACH BLUEBERRY CRISP WITH ALMOND TOPPING

 *Nothing spells summer like fresh peaches and juicy blueberries. This crisp recipe combines these two fabulous summer fruits with a crunchy almond-scented topping. Enjoy it with either a dollop of light whipped topping or a scoop of your favorite vanilla ice cream.*

3½ cups fresh peaches, peeled, sliced

2 cups fresh or frozen blueberries

1 tablespoon all-purpose flour

2 teaspoons lemon juice

¼ cup Splenda Granular

TOPPING

¼ cup old-fashioned oats

¼ cup all-purpose flour

¼ cup sliced almonds

½ cup Splenda Granular

4 tablespoons light butter

1. Preheat oven to 375°F.
2. In a 7 × 11-inch baking dish combine peaches, blueberries, flour, lemon juice, and Splenda. Set aside.
3. In small bowl combine oats, flour, almonds, and Splenda. Cut in butter and crumble on top of fruit mixture. Place in baking dish and bake 30–40 minutes.

Serves Eight (½ cup)

PER SERVING

Calories 130

Carbohydrate 22 grams

Protein 2 grams

Fat 5 grams (2 saturated)

Fiber 3 grams

Sodium 20 milligrams

Diabetic exchange = 1 Fruit, ½ Carbohydrate, ½ Fat

WW point comparison = 2 points

SWEET CHEESE STRUDEL

Sweet cheese strudels are a popular European tradition. This is nice on its own or dressed up with either Boysenberry Syrup (page 265) or Sweet Cherry Topping (page 270).

CHEESE FILLING

½ cup light tub-style cream cheese

⅓ cup Splenda Granular

2 tablespoons + 1 teaspoon cornstarch

1 egg yolk

1½ teaspoons vanilla extract

½ teaspoon grated lemon or orange zest

1 cup part-skim ricotta cheese, preferably without added gums or stabilizers

STRUDEL

6 sheets phyllo dough (14 x 18 inches), thaw if frozen

½ tablespoon butter, melted

Confectioners' sugar for dusting

1. In a small bowl combine cream cheese, Splenda, cornstarch, egg yolk, vanilla, and zest; mix until well combined. With a rubber spatula, gently fold in ricotta cheese just until combined.

2. Preheat oven to 350°F. Lightly spray baking sheet with nonstick cooking spray.

3. Unroll phyllo on the prepared baking sheet. Gently spoon the cheese filling in a long, 12 × 2-inch mound along one long edge of the phyllo layers, leaving a 2-inch border between the mound and the short edges of the phyllo. Fold up the long edge and loosely roll up the strudel. (Do not roll too tightly; the filling will expand during baking.) Set the strudel seam-side down on the baking sheet. Fold and tuck the open ends securely but not tightly beneath the roll.

4. Brush the strudel with 1½ tablespoon butter. With a sharp paring knife, make four short (1-inch) diagonal slashes along the top of the strudel to allow steam to escape. Bake for 35–40 minutes, or until the phyllo is golden brown. Carefully transfer the strudel to a wire rack and let cool completely. Just before serving, dust with confectioner's sugar.

Serves Six

PER SERVING

Calories 130   Fat 6 grams (2 saturated)
Carbohydrate 12 grams   Fiber 0 grams
Protein 6 grams   Sodium 190 milligrams

Diabetic exchange = 1 Carbohydrate, 1 Lean Meat, ½ Fat
WW point comparison = 2 points

 One ounce of cheese has as much calcium as 8 ounces of milk.

PHYLLO APPLE PACKETS

These delicious apple pastries are fancy enough for your next dinner party. Developed by pastry chef Laura Johanson, an apprentice of mine from the Culinary Institute of America, these all-purpose apple packets can be prepared in advance and placed in the oven to bake while you eat. They are an impressive hot dessert. Dust them lightly with powdered sugar for a beautiful presentation.

APPLE FILLING

2   **tablespoons butter**

2   **baking apples, diced (about ¾ pound)**

½   **cup Splenda Granular**

2   **teaspoons cinnamon**

4   **tablespoons lemon juice**

¼   **teaspoon salt**

6   **tablespoons unsweetened applesauce**

6   **sheets phyllo dough (12 x 16 inches)**

1. Preheat oven to 350°F. Lightly spray baking sheet with nonstick cooking spray.
2. In a medium frying pan melt butter on medium-high heat and toss in diced apples.
3. In a small mixing bowl combine Splenda, cinnamon, lemon juice, and salt. Pour mixture over cooking apples. Cook apples just until fork tender.
4. Spread a large piece of wax paper onto work surface. Carefully lay one piece of phyllo dough onto surface with short side closest to you. Lightly spray with cooking spray and fold in half lengthwise. Spray again and fold in half away from you. Cut off excess phyllo to create a 6 × 6-inch square.
5. Place 1 tablespoon applesauce into center of square. Top with 2 tablespoons of cooked apple mixture. Fold each corner to the middle, covering the apple filling while spraying lightly with cooking spray to hold edges together. Repeat 5 times.
6. With a spatula, carefully place packets on baking sheet. Bake for 25–30 minutes until golden brown.

Serves Six

PER SERVING

Calories 150

Fat 7 grams (2.5 saturated)

Carbohydrate 20 grams

Fiber 2 grams

Protein 1 gram

Sodium 115 milligrams

Diabetic exchange = 1 Fruit, ½ Carbohydrate, 1 Fat
WW point comparison = 3 points

Cakes and Cheesecakes

A BIRTHDAY WITHOUT A CAKE? WELL, I CAN'T EVEN THINK OF IT. SPECIAL occasions and cakes just go together, along with overindulgence in these traditionally rich and sugary treats. I recently saw a recipe for a cake where each piece contained over 800 calories and 100 (yes, that's 100) grams of carbohydrate. More surprising, it was not a gooey, obviously sugary cake, just a filled and frosted layer cake with a cup of sugar in the mixture and several more in the frosting—the type we have all made (and ate!). For richness it's cheesecake that takes the dubious prize, with over 50 grams of fat and 600 calories or more per piece! It is usually said that we can healthfully enjoy these treats "occasionally." But just how occasionally must that be? I have developed lots of great cakes and cheesecakes that are not *only* for special occasions. Because all of these "cakes" are low in sugar, fat, and calories, they can be enjoyed any time at all. In fact, if your idea of a special occasion is *everyday*, you can even wake up to a cheesecake for breakfast with Breakfast Cheesecake Cups. Enlightened versions of traditional homestyle cakes, like Pineapple Upside Down Cake, will brighten up the most ordinary days, while Chocolate Carrot Cake may very well become your next totable favorite. For special occasions I suggest one of the scrumptious filled cake rolls for a birthday (just line the candles up!) or a tangy Margarita Cheesecake for your next party (*olé*). And finally, because I love Christmas (and I love cheesecake), I developed the Black Forest Cheesecake Parfaits for only 200 calories, just for me (but I am willing to share).

CAKES AND CHEESECAKES

Chocolate Carrot Cake

Grandma's Gingerbread

Fruit Cocktail Snack Cake

Basic Yellow Cake

Pineapple Upside Down Cake

Cream Cheese Filled Pumpkin Roll

Chocolate Cake Roll with Chocolate Mousse Filling

Breakfast Cheesecake Cups

Everyday Cheesecake

Almond Orange Ricotta Cheesecake (No-Bake!)

Lemon Chiffon Cheesecake

Margarita Cheesecake

Cheesecake Squares

Black Forest Cheesecake Parfaits

CHOCOLATE CARROT CAKE

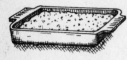

A novel twist on two favorites, this recipe combines the moist texture of traditional carrot cake with a delicious chocolate cake. It's easy to make and to tote. It appeals to both the chocolate lover and the health nut. Great for picnics and potlucks—no doubt it will be a hit wherever you go!

1⅔ cups all-purpose flour	1 large egg
⅓ cup cocoa powder	3 large egg whites
2½ teaspoons baking soda	1½ teaspoons vanilla extract
1 teaspoon baking powder	⅔ cup orange juice
1 teaspoon cinnamon	2 cups carrots, grated (about 3 medium)
1½ cups Splenda Granular	
¼ cup prune puree or 1 2.5-ounce jar baby food prunes	¼ cup coconut, shredded
	¼ cup pecan pieces
¼ cup canola oil	2 teaspoons powdered sugar (optional)

1. Preheat oven to 350°F. Coat a 9 × 13-inch cake pan with nonstick cooking spray.
2. In a medium bowl sift together flour, cocoa, baking soda, baking powder, and cinnamon. Add Splenda and set aside.
3. In a large mixing bowl whisk together prune puree, canola oil, egg, egg whites, vanilla extract, and orange juice.
4. Fold flour mixture into prune mixture ½ cup at a time. When all the flour is folded in, fold in carrots, and then pour batter into prepared pan.
5. Before baking, sprinkle coconut and pecans on top. Bake for 25-30 minutes. Cool and serve. Dust with powdered sugar if desired before serving.

Serves Sixteen

PER SERVING

Calories 140
Carbohydrate 18 grams
Protein 3 grams

Fat 6 grams (1 saturated)
Fiber 2 grams
Sodium 230 milligrams

Diabetic exchange = 1 Carbohydrate, 1 Fat
WW point comparison = 3 points

GRANDMA'S GINGERBREAD

Sweet accents of ginger and cinnamon combine with molasses to give this gingerbread its traditional old-fashioned flavor.

1 **cup all-purpose flour**	3 **tablespoons canola oil**
½ **cup whole wheat flour**	¼ **cup prune puree or**
1 **teaspoon ginger**	**1 2.5-ounce jar baby food**
1 **teaspoon cinnamon**	**prunes**
¼ **teaspoon cloves**	1 **large egg**
1 **teaspoon baking soda**	½ **cup water**
¼ **cup molasses**	½ **cup Splenda Granular**

1. Preheat oven to 350°F. Coat an 8-inch square cake pan with non-stick cooking spray.
2. In a medium bowl sift together flours, spices, and baking soda. Set aside.
3. In a large mixing bowl whisk together remaining ingredients.
4. Fold dry ingredients into molasses mixture and then pour batter into prepared pan. Bake for 18–20 minutes or until top springs back when touched. Cool and serve with light whipped topping if desired.

Serves Nine

PER SERVING

Calories 160	Fat 5 grams (0.5 saturated)
Carbohydrate 26 grams	Fiber 2 grams
Protein 3 grams	Sodium 150 milligrams

Diabetic exchange = 1½ Carbohydrate, 1 Fat
WW point comparison = 3 points

Molasses has a distinct flavor that brings depth of flavor and richness of color to many spice-laden recipes.

FRUIT COCKTAIL SNACK CAKE

This is a moist and tender, fruity and delicious snack cake. The key ingredient can be found in a can right in your cupboard. Make this snack cake on a moment's notice and you'll be sure to please your family and friends. Add a dollop of whipped topping to dress it up for a light summer dessert.

1 large egg	1 teaspoon baking powder
1 cup Splenda Granular	1 teaspoon baking soda
1 15-ounce can fruit cocktail, in light syrup (less 2 tablespoons juice)	½ teaspoon salt
	1¼ cups all-purpose flour
	1 teaspoon vanilla extract

1. Preheat oven to 325°F. Coat an 8-inch square cake pan with non-stick cooking spray.
2. In a large mixing bowl beat egg, Splenda, and fruit cocktail with a hand mixer until smooth.
3. In a medium bowl sift together dry ingredients.
4. Fold dry ingredients into fruit cocktail mixture with a whisk; then add vanilla extract.
5. Pour batter into prepared pan and bake for 30–35 minutes or until top springs back when touched. Cool and serve.

Serves Nine

PER SERVING

Calories 110
Carbohydrate 23 grams
Protein 3 grams

Fat 1 gram (0 saturated)
Fiber 1 gram
Sodium 200 milligrams

Diabetic exchange = 1 Carbohydrate, ½ Fruit
WW point comparison = 2 points

BASIC YELLOW CAKE

While developing the recipe for Pineapple Upside Down Cake (page 246), I discovered that even without the pineapple topping, the cake base was a winner. Simply dusted with powdered sugar, this cake is delicious. Use its wonderful light texture and golden appearance as a creative backdrop for your favorite toppings, textures, and flavors.

¼ cup butter, softened	1½ teaspoons baking powder
⅔ cup Splenda Granular	½ teaspoon baking soda
1 large egg	⅓ cup 1% milk
1 teaspoon vanilla extract	⅓ cup pineapple juice (may
1¼ cups all-purpose flour	substitute apple juice)

1. Preheat oven to 350°F. Coat an 8-inch round cake pan with non-stick cooking spray.
2. In a medium bowl with an electric mixer, cream butter and Splenda. Beat in egg and vanilla.
3. In a small bowl sift together dry ingredients.
4. Alternate mixing liquid and dry ingredients into creamed mixture.
5. Pour batter into prepared pan and bake 25–30 minutes or until top springs back when touched. Cool in pan on rack.

Serves Eight

PER SERVING

Calories 140
Carbohydrate 18 grams
Protein 3 grams

Fat 6 grams (1.5 saturated)
Fiber 1 gram
Sodium 230 milligrams

Diabetic exchange = 1 Carbohydrate, 1 Fat
WW point comparison = 3 points

Try adorning this with fresh sliced berries or Boysenberry Syrup (page 265).

PINEAPPLE UPSIDE DOWN CAKE

Truly a classic. Pineapple upside down cakes have been enjoyed for many generations. Some recipes call for as much as ¾ cup brown sugar and ½ stick of butter to be used for the topping alone. This version still retains the look and the taste of the sweet pineapple topping and offers a moist, tender cake, with only a fraction of the usual sugar and fat. Enjoy!

TOPPING

2 tablespoons butter
2 tablespoons brown sugar
¼ cup Splenda Granular
½ teaspoon cinnamon
6 pineapple rings

CAKE

¼ cup butter, softened

⅔ cup Splenda Granular
1 large egg
1 teaspoon vanilla extract
1¼ cups all-purpose flour
1½ teaspoons baking powder
½ teaspoon baking soda
⅓ cup 1% milk
⅓ cup pineapple juice

1. Preheat oven to 350°F. Coat an 8-inch round cake pan with non-stick cooking spray.
2. In oven, melt butter in prepared 8-inch pan. After butter is melted, evenly sprinkle with brown sugar, Splenda, and cinnamon. Arrange pineapple slices in pan. Set aside.
3. In a medium bowl with an electric mixer, cream butter and Splenda. Beat in egg and vanilla.
4. In a small bowl sift together dry ingredients. In another small bowl or liquid measure, combine milk and pineapple juice.
5. Alternate mixing liquid and dry ingredients into creamed mixture.
6. Pour batter over pineapple rings and bake 25–30 minutes. Turn cake out of pan. Cool on rack.

Serves Eight

PER SERVING

Calories 185
Carbohydrate 24 grams
Protein 3 grams

Fat 8 grams (2 saturated)
Fiber 1 gram
Sodium 260 milligrams

Diabetic exchange = 2 Fat, 1 Carbohydrate, ½ Fruit
WW point comparison = 4 points

In 1925, Dole Pineapple had a pineapple recipe contest. They received 2,500 recipes for pineapple upside down cake!

CREAM CHEESE FILLED PUMPKIN ROLL

Put this at the top of your list for holiday desserts. It is decorative, delicious, and definitely lights up any Thanksgiving or Christmas dessert table. Luscious with a cream cheese filling and spiced just right, it is sure to be a crowd-pleaser.

CAKE

3   large eggs
1   cup Splenda Granular
⅔   cup canned pumpkin
1   teaspoon molasses
1½ teaspoons cinnamon
½   teaspoon ginger
½   teaspoon nutmeg
¾   cup + 1 tablespoon all-purpose flour

1   teaspoon baking powder
¼   teaspoon baking soda

FILLING

8   ounces light cream cheese
3   tablespoons Splenda Granular
½   cup light whipped topping

2   teaspoons powdered sugar

1. Preheat oven to 350°F. Coat a 10 × 12-inch jelly roll or 9 × 13 × ½-inch cake pan with non-stick cooking spray. Line the bottom of the pan with wax paper and lightly spray wax paper with nonstick cooking spray. Set aside.
2. In a medium mixing bowl use electric mixer on high speed and beat eggs for 5 minutes; beat in Splenda. Whisk pumpkin, molasses, and spices into eggs.
3. Sift flour, baking powder, and baking soda into pumpkin mixture.
4. Pour batter into prepared pan. Using spatula, completely level batter. Bake for 8 minutes until cake is springy to the touch and edges appear dry. (Do not overbake or cake will crack when it is rolled.) Lay smooth towel onto work surface. Sift powdered sugar onto towel. As soon as cake comes out of oven, turn cake onto towel, and loosely roll up. Cool.
5. In a small mixing bowl beat light cream cheese and Splenda with a hand mixer. Beat in whipped topping.
6. Unroll cooled cake. Spread filling over cake, stopping 1 inch from the farthest long side. Starting from the long side closest to you, reroll cake. Cover with plastic wrap and refrigerate cake until ready to serve. Dust with powdered sugar before serving if desired.

Serves Eight

PER SERVING

Calories 170

Carbohydrate 18 grams

Protein 7 grams

Fat 7 grams (4 saturated)

Fiber 1 gram

Sodium 310 milligrams

Diabetic exchange = 1 Carbohydrate, 1 Fat, 1 Lean Meat

WW point comparison = 4 points

 Be sure to use the correct size pan, spread the batter evenly, and roll the cake while still warm to avoid cracking.

CHOCOLATE CAKE ROLL WITH CHOCOLATE MOUSSE FILLING

"Yule logs"—traditionally, rich and moist cake rolls filled with buttercream and adorned with rich chocolate frosting—are often served at the holidays. The traditional version is deceptively "light" but is actually weighed down by an enormous amount of sugar and fat. In contrast, I have created this moist chocolate sponge cake filled and rolled with a rich chocolate mousse filling that is heavy only in taste.

CAKE
1/3 cup Dutch-processed cocoa
1/3 cup water
3 eggs, separated
1/2 cup Splenda Granular
1/4 cup prune puree or 1 2.5-ounce jar baby food prunes
1/2 teaspoon vanilla
1/2 cup cake flour
2 egg whites
1/2 teaspoon cream of tartar
2 tablespoons granulated sugar

2 teaspoons cocoa powder (for rolling)

FILLING
1/2 cup light tub-style cream cheese
2 cups light whipped topping
1/4 cup Dutch-process cocoa powder
1/2 cup Splenda Granular
1/2 teaspoon vanilla extract
1 teaspoon powdered sugar (optional)

1. Preheat oven to 350°F. Coat a 10 × 12-inch jelly roll or 9 × 13 × 1/2-inch cake pan with nonstick cooking spray. Line the bottom of the pan with wax paper and lightly spray wax paper with non-stick cooking spray. Set aside.
2. In a small bowl dissolve cocoa in water. Beat yolks with Splenda until thick and fluffy (about 5 minutes). Add dissolved cocoa, prune puree, and vanilla to beaten yolks. Sift half the flour over egg mixture and fold it in gently with balloon whisk or rubber spatula. Repeat with remaining flour.
3. Beat egg whites until foamy, add cream of tartar, and beat until soft peaks form. Beat in granulated sugar until stiff peaks form. Fold egg whites into batter and pour batter into prepared pan. Use spatula to completely level batter.
4. Bake for 18–21 minutes until cake is springy to the touch. (Do not overbake or the cake will crack when it is rolled.) Lay smooth

towel onto work surface. Sift cocoa powder onto towel. Allow cake to cool in pan 2–4 minutes. Turn cake onto towel, and loosely roll up. Cool.

5. In a medium bowl with an electric mixer beat cream cheese until smooth. Beat in whipped topping, cocoa powder, Splenda, and vanilla until smooth and fluffy.

6. Unroll cooled cake. Spread filling over cake, stopping 1 inch from the farthest short side. Starting from the short side closest to you, roll cake up again. Cover with plastic wrap and refrigerate cake until ready to serve. Dust with powdered sugar before serving if desired.

Serves Eight

PER SERVING

Calories 200
Carbohydrate 24 grams
Protein 7 grams

Fat 7 grams (4.5 saturated)
Fiber 2 grams
Sodium 120 milligrams

Diabetic exchange = 1½ Carbohydrate, 1 Lean Meat, 1 Fat
WW point comparison = 4 points

See pumpkin roll (page 247) for cake roll tips.

BREAKFAST CHEESECAKE CUPS

What could be better than cheesecake for breakfast? These creamy orange-scented cheesecake cups have as much protein as two eggs—with less fat and calories. What a sweet way to start your day.

2 cups 1% cottage cheese	½ teaspoon almond extract
8 ounces tub-style light cream cheese, room temperature	½ teaspoon orange zest
	2 large eggs
⅔ cup Splenda Granular	2 large egg whites

1. Preheat oven to 350°F. Set seven 6-ounce custard cups in a large baking pan (with at least 2-inch sides).
2. In a food processor, puree cottage cheese until *completely* smooth. Add cream cheese, Splenda, almond extract, and orange zest; process until smooth. Add eggs and egg whites, one at a time; process to incorporate.
3. Pour mixture into custard cups. Add hot water to pan until halfway up sides of custard cups. Bake for 25–30 minutes or until set in center. Chill for at least 4 hours. Serve.

Serves Seven (½ cup)

PER SERVING

Calories 130
Carbohydrate 6 grams
Protein 14 grams

Fat 8 grams (4 saturated)
Fiber 0 grams
Sodium 380 milligrams

Diabetic exchange = 2 Lean Meat, ½ Carbohydrate
WW point comparison = 3 points

Adding protein to your breakfast will help keep you satisfied longer and keep your blood sugar on an even keel.

EVERYDAY CHEESECAKE

People usually think of cheesecakes as only for special occasions. This cheese-cake, however, is so healthy and simple to make that there is no reason not to enjoy it every day. I have streamlined the steps and bake it in a regular 8-inch cake pan.

CRUST
1 tablespoon butter, melted
½ cup graham-cracker crumbs
2 tablespoons Splenda Granular

FILLING
8 ounces lowfat cottage cheese
8 ounces nonfat cream cheese, room temperature
8 ounces light tub-style cream cheese, room temperature

1 cup Splenda Granular
2 tablespoons cornstarch
2 tablespoons all-purpose flour
  Zest of one lemon
1 teaspoon vanilla extract
2 large eggs
2 large egg whites
1 cup sour cream

1. Preheat oven to 350°F. Coat an 8-inch round cake pan with non-stick cooking spray.
2. Place melted butter in cake pan. Toss in graham-cracker crumbs and Splenda. Using your hand, mix and pat onto bottom of pan. Set crust in oven for 10 minutes. Cool completely. Place pan in a 9 × 13-inch or larger baking pan with 2–3-inch sides.
3. Place cottage cheese in a food processor or blender. Puree until completely smooth. Spoon into a large mixing bowl and add cream cheeses. Beat on medium speed with an electric mixer until creamy. Add Splenda, cornstarch, flour, zest, and vanilla. Beat on low until smooth. Add eggs, and then egg whites, beating briefly after each addition to incorporate. Fold in sour cream.
4. Pour mixture into set crust. Place cheesecake into large, deep baking pan and add hot water to reach halfway up sides of cake pan. Bake in water bath for 50–55 minutes or until sides of cake appear firm and center is barely set. Remove from water bath and cool. Chill at least 6 hours before serving.

Serves Twelve

PER SERVING

Calories 160
Carbohydrate 13 grams
Protein 10 grams

Fat 7 grams (4.5 saturated)
Fiber 0 grams
Sodium 330 milligrams

Diabetic exchange = 1½ Lean Meat, 1 Carbohydrate
WW point comparison = 4 points

To dress this cake up for any occasion, bake in a springform pan and be sure to wrap it in heavy-duty aluminum foil prior to placing it in the water bath. Use your choice of sauce or topping from the Sweet Endings section of the book.

ALMOND ORANGE RICOTTA CHEESECAKE (NO-BAKE!)

This no-bake cheesecake is lovely. Scented with orange and sitting pretty on an almond shortbread crust, it is truly perfect for summer. Unlike many ricotta cheesecakes, this is smooth and creamy rather than dry.

CRUST

1/3 cup all-purpose flour

3 tablespoons finely chopped almonds (about 1/4 cup whole)

2 tablespoons Splenda Granular

2 1/2 teaspoons margarine or butter

2/3 cup Splenda Granular

1 tablespoon vanilla extract

2 teaspoons orange extract

1 teaspoon lemon zest

8 ounces evaporated or skim milk

FILLING

2 1/2 envelopes unflavored gelatin

1/4 cup cold water

2 cups part-skim ricotta cheese

TOPPING

2 tablespoons sliced almonds

1 teaspoon granulated sugar (optional)

1. Coat an 8-inch round cake pan with nonstick cooking spray.
2. In a small bowl mix flour, almonds, and Splenda. Cut in margarine with a fork or fingers until mixture resembles coarse crumbs. Pat crust into prepared pan.
3. In a small bowl sprinkle gelatin over water. Set aside.
4. Puree the ricotta in a food processor and add Splenda with extracts and zest.
5. In a small saucepan simmer evaporated milk until bubbles appear on rim of pot; pull off heat. Whisk in gelatin. Pour into food processor and blend with the ricotta mixture.
6. Pour cheesecake batter into prepared crust. Refrigerate until set (at least 4 hours). Sprinkle almonds around outside rim of cake. Sprinkle sugar on top of almonds (it makes them sparkle) if desired.

Serves Ten

PER SERVING

Calories 170
Carbohydrate 11 grams
Protein 10 grams

Fat 9 grams (3 saturated)
Fiber 0 grams
Sodium 120 milligrams

Diabetic exchange = 1 1/2 Lean Meat, 1 Carbohydrate, 1 Fat
WW point comparison = 4 points

A twist of orange placed right in the middle of the cake is the perfect adornment.

LEMON CHIFFON CHEESECAKE

Light and luscious, this recipe was inspired by one I once ate at a famous cheesecake restaurant. I was impressed with how light and chiffonlike it was. After several trials, I came up with a baked cheesecake that I enjoyed just as much. This is one of my favorite endings to a delicious and elegant meal.

CRUST

¾ cup graham-cracker crumbs

2 tablespoons Splenda Granular

2 tablespoons butter, melted

FILLING

1 cup 1% cottage cheese

8 ounces light tub-style cream cheese, room temperature

8 ounces fat-free cream cheese, room temperature

1¼ cups Splenda Granular

1 tablespoon cornstarch

1 tablespoon all-purpose flour

2 large egg yolks

¼ cup lemon juice

1 tablespoon lemon zest

4 large egg whites

1. Preheat oven to 350°F. Coat a 9-inch springform pan with nonstick cooking spray. Wrap pan tightly with heavy-duty aluminum foil to make waterproof

2. In a small bowl mix together graham cracker crumbs, Splenda, and melted butter. Pat into the bottom of a prepared 9-inch round cake pan. Bake crust in oven for 10 minutes. Cool completely. Place pan in a 9 × 13-inch or larger baking pan with 2–3 inch sides.

3. Place cottage cheese in a food processor or blender. Puree until completely smooth. Spoon into a large mixing bowl and add cream cheeses. Beat on medium speed with an electric mixer until creamy. Add Splenda, cornstarch, flour, egg yolks, lemon juice, and zest. In a large mixing bowl, whip egg whites. Fold beaten whites into cheese mixture. Pour cheesecake batter into prepared crust.

4. Pour hot water into baking pan to reach halfway up sides of cake pan. Bake in water bath for 50–55 minutes or until sides of cake appear firm and center is barely set. Remove from water bath and cool. Chill at least 6 hours before serving.

Serves Twelve

Per Serving

Calories 140

Carbohydrate 11 grams

Protein 10 grams

Fat 6 grams (3.5 saturated)

Fiber 0 grams

Sodium 340 milligrams

Diabetic exchange = 1½ Lean Meat, 1 Carbohydrate

WW point comparison = 3 points

MARGARITA CHEESECAKE

Next time you're sipping a frosty margarita, imagine that refreshingly cool flavor blended into a creamy, sweet cheesecake. The thumbs-up was given to this recipe by my neighbors who thought it succeeded in doing just that! So, why not head south of the border with a slice of this very adult-flavored cheesecake? What a great party pleaser.

CRUST
¾ cup graham-cracker crumbs
2 tablespoons butter, melted
2 tablespoons Splenda Granular

FILLING
8 ounces 1% cottage cheese
8 ounces light tub-style cream cheese, room temperature
8 ounces fat-free cream cheese, room temperature

1 cup light sour cream
1 cup Splenda Granular
2 large eggs
3 large egg whites
2 tablespoons tequila
2 tablespoons triple sec
2 tablespoons fresh lime juice

TOPPING
2 tablespoons graham-cracker crumbs
1 tablespoon Splenda Granular

1. Preheat oven to 350°F. Coat a 9-inch springform pan with nonstick cooking spray. Wrap pan tightly with heavy-duty aluminum foil to make waterproof.
2. In a small bowl mix together graham-cracker crumbs, melted butter, and Splenda. Pat into the bottom of a prepared 9-inch round pan. Bake crust in oven for 10 minutes. Cool completely. Place pan in a 9 × 13-inch or larger baking pan with 2–3 inch sides.
3. Place cottage cheese in a food processor or blender. Puree until completely smooth. Spoon into a large mixing bowl and add cream cheeses. Beat on medium speed with an electric mixer until creamy. Add sour cream and Splenda and beat until smooth. Beat in eggs and whites one at a time. Stir in tequila, triple sec and lime juice. Pour cheesecake batter into prepared crust.
4. Pour hot water into baking pan to reach halfway up sides of cake pan. Bake in water bath for 50–55 minutes just until set in center. Combine graham-cracker crumbs and Splenda and sprinkle on top. Remove from water bath. Chill and serve.

Serves Twelve

PER SERVING

Calories 170

Carbohydrate 14 grams

Protein 9 grams

Fat 6 grams (3.5 saturated)

Fiber 0 grams

Sodium 340 milligrams

Diabetic exchange = 1½ Lean Meat, 1 Carbohydrate

WW point comparison = 3 points

 Contrary to popular belief, tequila is not made from cactus. It is made from the blue agave, which is a member of the lily family.

CHEESECAKE SQUARES

Virginia, from Toronto, Canada, sent me her original cheesecake recipe. I've taken out the sugar and you can't even tell the difference! These creamy, sweet squares, placed on a large platter topped with sour cream and garnished with slices of fresh strawberries, are perfect for entertaining family and friends. Virginia says they are always a hit!

CRUST

1¼ cups graham-cracker crumbs

2 tablespoons margarine or butter, melted

½ teaspoon cinnamon

2 tablespoon Splenda Granular

FILLING

2 8-ounce packages light cream cheese, room temperature

1 8-ounce package fat-free cream cheese, room temperature

3 large eggs

2 tablespoons lemon juice

2 tablespoons lemon zest

2 teaspoons vanilla

1 cup Splenda Granular

TOPPING

2 cups reduced-fat sour cream

½ cup Splenda Granular

2 teaspoons vanilla

1. Preheat oven to 325°F.
2. In a small bowl combine graham cracker crumbs, margarine, cinnamon, and Splenda; stir. Pour crumb mixture into 9 × 13-inch pan. With your fingers, the back of a spoon, or a sheet of plastic wrap, press down on the crumbs until they coat the bottom and sides of the pan. Refrigerate at least 30 minutes.
3. Using an electric mixer, beat cream cheeses, eggs, lemon juice, lemon zest, vanilla, and Splenda. Pour into refrigerated crust. Bake 20–25 minutes. Remove from oven. Cool 10 minutes. Increase oven temperature to 400°F.
4. For topping, in medium bowl combine sour cream, Splenda, and vanilla. Spread on slightly cooled cheesecake. Bake additional 5–8 minutes to set topping. Cool and chill at least 4 hours before serving.
5. Cut cheesecake into 24 squares (6 × 4).

FRUIT GARNISH VARIATION: Serve cheesecake squares in decorative paper cupcake cups and top with slices of fresh kiwi, strawberry halves, or candied cherries cut into quarters.

RASPBERRY SAUCE VARIATION: Combine 3 tablespoons low-sugar raspberry jam, 3 tablespoons water, and ¼ cup Splenda in a microwavable bowl. Heat for 15–30 seconds on high. Stir until smooth, and splatter on top of cheesecake with a fork before slicing cheesecake into squares.

Serves Twenty-four

PER SERVING

Calories 120
Carbohydrate 7 grams
Protein 5 grams

Fat 7 grams (4 saturated)
Fiber 0 grams
Sodium 160 milligrams

Diabetic exchange = 1 Lean Meat, 1 Fat, ½ Carbohydrate
WW point comparison = 3 points

BLACK FOREST CHEESECAKE PARFAITS

These cheesecake parfaits are a variation of a version found in my first book, made with regular graham-cracker crumbs and blueberries. These cheesecakes are just as delicious to eat as they are unique and impressive to serve. They are fabulous for entertaining as they are already portioned and can be made ahead of time.

1½ cups frozen black cherries, thawed

2 tablespoons Splenda Granular

½ teaspoon almond extract

½ cup chocolate graham-cracker crumbs

2 tablespoons Splenda Granular

1½ tablespoons cocoa powder

½ tablespoon butter, melted

4 ounces light tub-style cream cheese, room temperature

4 ounces fat-free cream cheese, room temperature

½ cup light sour cream

¼ cup Splenda Granular

1½ cups light whipped topping

1. Select 6 tall stemmed glasses (an 8-ounce wineglass or champagne glass is ideal). In a small bowl mix cherries, 2 tablespoons Splenda, and almond extract. Set aside.
2. In a small bowl mix graham-cracker crumbs, 2 tablespoons Splenda, cocoa powder, and butter. Set aside.
3. In a medium mixing bowl beat cream cheeses with an electric mixer until creamy. Add sour cream and Splenda and stir until smooth. Fold in whipped topping with a spoon or spatula. In the bottom of each glass, place 1 tablespoon graham-cracker mix. Press down with spoon. Place about 3 tablespoons of cream cheese mix on top of each. (You will use only half of the cheese mixture for the 6 glasses.) Divide the cherries among the glasses, placing them on top of the cream cheese layer. Add one more layer of cream cheese. Finish the parfait by topping each with 1 tablespoon of crumbs.
4. These can be enjoyed immediately, or place them in the refrigerator until you are ready to serve them.

Serves Six

PER SERVING

Calories 200
Carbohydrate 24 grams
Protein 7 grams

Fat 8 grams (2 saturated)
Fiber 1 gram
Sodium 290 milligrams

Diabetic exchange = 1½ Carbohydrate, 1 Lean Meat, 1 Fat
WW point comparison = 4 points

 The name "Black Forest" originated in the Black Forest region of Germany, where the delectable combination of chocolate, whipped cream, and sour cherries was originally used in a torte.

Sweet Endings

LAST, BUT CERTAINLY NOT LEAST, I OFFER SWEET ENDINGS. EVER SO VERSATILE, these "endings" add the perfect touch to whatever they grace. The uses for them are practically, well, endless. I picture the Apple Butter Syrup sprucing up ordinary frozen waffles and the Boysenberry Sauce turning a plain piece of cake into something spectacular. I envision French toast all jazzed up when served with bourbon sauce and store-bought Angel Food Cake ethereal when topped with Sun Sweet Orange Sauce for a quick dessert. I also see the smiles of delight as someone receives jars of Sweet Cherry Topping and Crunchy Cinnamon Pecans to use on cheesecakes and ice cream. And I dream of a piece of Chocolate Cream Filled Chocolate Roll sitting in a pool of Dark Chocolate Sauce. Before I get any more carried away, let me just say the only limit for these terrific low-sugar embellishments is your own imagination!

SWEET ENDINGS

Boysenberry Syrup
Apple Cider Butter Syrup
Sun Sweet Orange Sauce
Bourbon Sauce
Dark Chocolate Sauce
Sweet Cherry Topping
Crunchy Cinnamon Pecans

BOYSENBERRY SYRUP

While developing the recipe for Buttermilk Boysenberry Sherbet, I just so happened to get a spoonful of the boysenberry and sugar syrup mixture in my mouth. It tasted wonderful and inspired me to develop this boysenberry syrup that can also be used on pancakes, cakes, and frozen desserts. The visual effect of this dark purple syrup drizzled over plain cheesecake is especially dramatic and will dazzle your guests.

½ cup Splenda Granular

½ cup water

1 12-ounce bag (about 2 cups) frozen boysenberries, partially thawed

2 teaspoons cornstarch + 2 tablespoons cold water

1. In a medium saucepan heat Splenda and water over medium heat. Bring to simmer and add boysenberries. Cook for 5 minutes. Remove from heat and strain through a sieve; pressing down on berries with the back of a spoon to force pulp through sieve. Return syrup to pan and add cornstarch mixture. Heat until mixture thickens and clears. Mixture will thicken further on cooling.

Serves Twelve (2 tablespoons)

PER SERVING

Calories 25
Carbohydrate 6 grams
Protein 0 grams

Fat 0 grams (0 saturated)
Fiber 1 gram
Sodium 0 milligrams

Diabetic exchange = Free
WW point comparison = 0 points

APPLE CIDER BUTTER SYRUP

Here is a delicious alternative that has only a fraction of the sugar of traditional syrup, proving that syrups don't have to be sweet, sticky concoctions that add undue sugar and calories to already high-calorie foods.

¾ **cup apple cider**
½ **cup Splenda Granular**
1 **teaspoon cornstarch +**
    2 teaspoons cold water
1 **tablespoon butter**

1. In a small saucepan simmer apple cider and Splenda over medium heat until it reduces by one-third (to about ½ cup). Mix in cornstarch and water and bring to low boil; stir until syrup clears. Whisk in butter.

Serves Four (2 tablespoons)

PER SERVING

Calories 60
Carbohydrate 9 grams
Protein 0 grams

Fat 3 grams (2 saturated)
Fiber 0 grams
Sodium 25 milligrams

Diabetic exchange = ½ Fruit
WW point comparison = 1 point

Compare this to 2 tablespoons of maple syrup plus 1 pat of butter at 140 calories and 28 grams of carbohydrate.

SUN SWEET ORANGE SAUCE

If you like lemon curd, you'll love this sauce! With its twist of orange and unique creamy texture, you can top cakes, cheesecakes, or for something different, try it on your next batch of French toast. Originally made to adorn an orange "princess" cake, you'll find this sauce is truly fit for royalty.

2 large egg yolks	1 tablespoon orange zest
½ cup Splenda Granular	(about 1 orange)
Juice of 2 oranges	¼ teaspoon salt
(about 3/4 cup)	1 tablespoon butter, softened

1. In a small saucepan or double boiler combine yolks and Splenda. Whisk until Splenda dissolves.
2. Whisk in orange juice, zest, and salt. Place saucepan on low heat and cook until mixture coats the back of a spoon. Remove from heat, and stir in butter. Chill.

Serves Six

PER SERVING

Calories 20
Carbohydrate 2 grams
Protein 2 grams

Fat 2 grams (1 saturated)
Fiber 0 grams
Sodium 35 milligrams

Diabetic exchange = Free
WW point comparison = ½ point

If you don't have a double boiler, use this trick: thoroughly whisk all ingredients together in the saucepan before placing it onto gentle heat.

BOURBON SAUCE

This sauce was created for the New Orleans Bread Pudding (page 186) but is a real keeper on its own. Spiked with real bourbon, you can use it over French toast to "kick it up a notch"—your brunch guests will love you for it!

6 tablespoons fat-free half-and-half	**2** teaspoons cornstarch
6 tablespoons low-fat milk	**2** tablespoons bourbon
¼ cup Splenda Granular	½ teaspoon vanilla
	1½ tablespoons butter, softened

1. In a small saucepan whisk together half-and-half, milk, Splenda, and cornstarch until smooth. Place over medium heat and cook, stirring, until mixture comes to a low boil and thickens. Whisk in bourbon, vanilla, and butter and immediately remove from heat. Serve sauce warm.

Serves Eight (2 tablespoons)

PER SERVING

Calories 45
Carbohydrate 3 grams
Protein 1 gram

Fat 2.5 grams (1.5 saturated)
Fiber 0 grams
Sodium 30 milligrams

Diabetic exchange = ½ Fat
WW point comparison = 1 point

For a nonalcoholic version, substitute orange juice for bourbon. It will impart a delicious, light orange accent.

DARK CHOCOLATE SAUCE

Deep, dark, and delicious, you are certain to find many uses for this oh-so-chocolaty sauce (even if it's only on a spoon!). Regular chocolate sauce recipes use melted chocolate, half-and-half, sugar, and corn syrup. I use similar elements in this sauce, retaining just enough of the corn syrup and melted chocolate to ensure a rich, smooth taste.

¼ **cup Dutch-processed cocoa powder,**

⅓ **cup Splenda Granular**

¼ **cup water**

⅓ **cup fat-free half-and-half**

I **tablespoon light corn syrup**

I **ounce semisweet chocolate, chopped**

I **teaspoon vanilla**

1. Combine cocoa, Splenda, water, half-and-half, and corn syrup in a small saucepan. Whisk over low heat until mixture is smooth and hot. (Do not boil.)
2. Remove from heat and whisk in chocolate and vanilla until chocolate melts and sauce is smooth again.

Serves Eight (2 tablespoons)

PER SERVING

Calories 45
Carbohydrate 8 grams
Protein I gram

Fat 2 grams (I saturated)
Fiber I gram
Sodium 15 milligrams

Diabetic exchange = ½ Carbohydrate
WW point comparison = I point

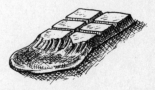

Americans consumed over 3.1 billion pounds of chocolate in 2001; almost half of the world's total production.

SWEET CHERRY TOPPING

Canned cherry pie filling pales in comparison to this recipe bursting with plump cherries and fresh orange peel. This topping is as good as any found in a gourmet food market. It also makes a perfect gift in a jar for Christmas—just the thing for someone who is watching the sugar in their diet.

16 ounces (about 3 cups) frozen dark cherries, slightly thawed
⅔ cup Splenda Granular
¾ cup water
1 tablespoon cornstarch

2 tablespoons orange liqueur or brandy
½ teaspoon vanilla
½ teaspoon almond extract
1–2 tablespoons orange peel (thin strips)

1. Place cherries in a medium saucepan. Add Splenda, water, and cornstarch and stir. Place on medium heat and cook slowly for 5 minutes or until cherries are warm. Turn heat up and bring to a low boil; cook, stirring just until mixture clears and sauce is thickened. Stir in liqueur and cook 1 minute.
2. Remove from heat and stir in vanilla, almond extract, and orange peel. Cool slightly and spoon into container.

Serves Eight (¼ cup)

PER SERVING

Calories 50
Carbohydrate 9 grams
Protein 1 gram

Fat 0 grams (0 saturated)
Fiber 1 gram
Sodium 0 milligrams

Diabetic exchange = ½ Carbohydrate
WW point comparison = 1 point

When in the freezer section, look for black cherries (not sour red cherries) for best results.

CRUNCHY CINNAMON PECANS

These pecans are great Christmas gifts. Your friends and family will never believe there is no sugar in these nuts. The heated egg white mixture provides the perfect foundation for the sweet cinnamon mixture to enrobe the pecans. Don't forget to try the spicy Cajun version—you won't believe how great they taste on vanilla ice cream.

1 large egg white
½ cup Splenda Granular
2 cups pecans
1 tablespoon cinnamon

1. Preheat oven to 350°F. Lightly spray baking sheet with nonstick cooking spray.
2. Beat egg white and Splenda together in a double boiler over medium heat. Remove from heat. Toss pecans in egg white mixture and add cinnamon. Spread coated pecans onto prepared sheet pan.
3. Bake at 350°F for 15 minutes, mixing nuts after baking halfway. Cool and serve.

SPICY CAJUN VARIATION: Substitute 1 tablespoon Cajun spice for the cinnamon.

Serves Eight (about 1 ounce)

PER SERVING

Calories 200
Carbohydrate 6 grams
Protein 3 grams

Fat 19 grams (2 saturated)
Fiber 2 grams
Sodium 5 milligrams

Diabetic exchange = 1 Fat
WW point comparison = 1 point

Index

About the Author

MARLENE KOCH, RD, author of the best-selling dessert book *Unbelievable Desserts with Splenda: Sweet Treats Low in Sugar, Fat, and Calories* is a culinary consultant and professional educator who specializes in good food and good health. In combining her love for great-tasting food with her knowledge of nutrition, she has become a popular teacher for the American Culinary Federation (the national association of chefs) and professional cooking schools as well as a frequent guest of network television and radio programs. Marlene's knowledge and enthusiasm have also been used on behalf of numerous public and professional organizations, including the Ohio News Network, the American Diabetes Association, the American Heart Association, and publications such as public television's chef George Hirsch's book *Living It Up* and *Cooking Light* and *Diabetic Cooking* magazines. Marlene can be found in Saratoga, California, soaking up the sun with her husband and two energetic young sons or on the Web at www.marlenekoch.com.

Illustrator CHRISTOPHER DOLLBAUM holds a master's degree in Fine Arts from the University of Washington, in Seattle, where he currently resides. He is known for his work in ceramic sculpture as well as his fine drawings.